ROSES ROUND THE DOOR

The Great Cottage Dream

BERWICK COATES

Published by Berwick Coates

Publishing partner: Paragon Publishing, Rothersthorpe

First published 2020

ISBN 978-1-78222-717-5

All illustrations by Berwick Coates

Book design, layout and production management by Into Print
www.intoprint.net
01604 832149

Dedication

To all those who dream of
a country cottage, and to those (not quite so many)
who achieve it.

INTRODUCTION

As I hinted in the Dedication, one of the commonest dreams of those who do not live in a cottage in the country is to do just that.

The fact that those dreams may not be very well-informed or practical does not detract from their intensity and vividness. Any more than those of the small boy who wants to be an astronaut, or the teenage girl who wants to be a pop star.

I was lucky. Twice over. Firstly because I did it, and secondly because I wasn't even trying at the time. It just sort of happened. This book is an account of *how* it happened, and what happened when it did happen.

Contents

Chapter

1

Finding

'Go and have a look. I think he's there.' The man took away my empty cup and plate and nodded towards the road rising up the slope from his house. 'It's not far. The bus stops up there anyway.'

Well, why not? I had an hour to wait. There was nothing else to do.

I duly walked up the gentle gradient – no trouble after three days traipsing and camping all over Exmoor. I was at least fit, if rather tired. The pack on the back was getting lighter at the prospect of dumping it beside me on the bus.

I found the turning easily enough. A short path climbed to a disused railway bridge, and then dipped sharply on the other side, down an overgrown path towards a valley. I hid the pack in some undergrowth, and began the descent.

I felt a bit sheepish. This was ridiculous. I wasn't even sure that there was a cottage down there at all. I had only the tea man's word for it. Then why would he think it worthwhile to deceive me?

But even if he was honest, what was I doing here? Going to look at a country cottage, for God's sake. With what purpose? I didn't have the money to buy one. Even if I did, I did not have the knowledge, or the time, to 'do it up'. I had a living to earn, and it certainly did not provide the opportunity, or the surplus, for rural real estate.

However, like so many thousands of city-dwellers, or more likely suburb-dwellers, I had this dream. It involved nebulous, mist-shrouded images of chattering streams, low lintels, mellowed stone, and hollyhocks round the door. Oh – and those windows criss-crossed with diamond-patterned lead calms, behind which genteel ladies like Beatrix Potter must have put out milk for the cat. (She could hardly have written about Peter Rabbit and Mrs. Tiggywinkle in a modern terrace council house, could she?)

However, there was one item which *was* no dream – the quiet. Well, sort of. As with most things connected with nature (nature in England, which does not boast continent-wide deserts or multi-thousand-metre mountains), there was in fact quite a lot to listen to if you took the trouble to stop and cock an ear – hedgerow trees rustlings in a breeze, bird calls, a tractor in a nearby field, a lorry on a distant road, even the tread of your own feet. But, no matter how individual, varied, or busy, it could never be described as intrusive. On the contrary, after the cacophony of a city street or a suburban crossroads or an adjacent airport, it was positively therapeutic. I could afford that all right. It was free. And I didn't need any specialised knowledge to be able to enjoy it.

So, almost before I knew it, I was well below the level of the road I had turned from, and out of sight of it. Nothing but double-rutted tractor track and brambling hedge, crowded cow-parsley and spring-sharpened nettles. There was a bend coming, and I thought I would get round that, and then go back to the bus stop. I glanced at my watch. Plenty of time yet, but it was as well to be prudent. Buses round here didn't come along as frequently as the 77A to Wimbledon.

Then I saw him. A man of indeterminate middle age, in a dark blue short-sleeved shirt and enormously baggy khaki shorts. The sort that British soldiers had to wear if they were posted anywhere vaguely tropical. I believe they were in fact christened 'Empire-builder's shorts'. Officers, thanks to batmen, had their shorts pressed and starched, so that they stuck out at the sides like flippers – right down to bony pink knees. Honestly, looking back, it's a wonder that the Zulus and Matabeles took them seriously – just the sight of them.

Anyway, there he was, trimming a hedge with a venerable sickle. So that made him at once someone with an interest in the place. He did not look like a council worker. His spare frame and slightly beaky nose marked him as vaguely scholarly. And the shorts too; there was no way he could be a farm tenant; he had to be an owner. Elementary, Watson; when you have eliminated the impossible, whatever remains must be the truth.

He paused in relief. I stopped, too – naturally. It would have been almost impossible to pass each other in that constricted lane without speaking. Even for unintroduced Englishmen.

And he was *very* English. That became evident as soon as he opened his mouth. His accent had public school written all over it. He might have been wearing a Charterhouse tie. It was Clifton actually, as I soon discovered. I was right about the shorts too; he was a retired Army officer.

So we began a predictable conversation. Was there a cottage down there at the bottom of the lane? Yes, indeed there was. Did he own it? Yes, he did. Was it a holiday cottage? Yes, he supposed you could call it that.

I forgot all my self-imposed common sense of five minutes ago, and began putting into vague words my even vaguer aspirations about the mellowed stone and the hollyhocks round the door. I have no idea how soppy it must have sounded, but he was too much of a gentleman to show that that was what he thought.

Yes, he said, he had been on a country walk (like the one I had just finished), and had passed it on the way back to the bus stop (just like me). He must have been very taken with it, because he gave up his bus, and took steps to make enquiries and find out who the owner was. I think my man with the tea was able to tell him. It was a local farmer.

He volunteered the information about the price, because *I* was too much of a gentleman to ask.

'Seven hundred and fifty.'

Seven hundred and fifty! And he meant pounds, not thousands. This was the 1960's. Even as far back as that, my general knowledge exceeded my dream capacity enough to know that it was an impossibly frugal figure. There must have been extraordinary circumstances. But there it was: I could see no reason why he should have lied to me, any more than the tea man would have lied to me about there being a cottage there at all. A country cottage for seven hundred and fifty pounds. My imagination was up and running again. . .

Luckily, my watch told me that it was time to go, before I launched into yet more romantic, 'wouldn't-it-be-nice' dreaming. I wished him goodbye, with regret, climbed back to the top of the hill, retrieved my pack, went back over the derelict bridge, and, just in time, hailed the low-slung green single-decker that grumbled up the slope with commendable punctuality.

Well, it had been nice while it lasted.

*

Three weeks later, I received a letter.

It was from the man with the sickle and the sticky-out shorts. He had acquired my address from the tea man up the road. I had forgotten, but it appeared that I had made an even bigger idiot of myself than I thought, and had left him my address, on the (zillions to one) offchance that a country cottage in the area might become available. Even at this distance of time, I blush at my Toad-like wishful thinking and impracticality.

Be that as it may, my sticky-out shorts man had had a conversation with the tea man (after all, they were sort of neighbours). And there was the letter. It contained an astounding offer.

He (the shorts man, not the tea man) had bought the cottage three or four years before, with a view to renovating it, naturally. But it had more accommodation that he really needed. If I was prepared to give a hand with this 'renovation', I could rent one half of it. Because it was still in a rudimentary state, he would not ask much in the way of rent, so long, as he said, I was willing to do my bit towards the improvements. Would I regard two pounds a week as reasonable?

Two pounds a week!

If I should happen to be interested in the project, perhaps I should like to come down, stay the night, look over the place, and maybe take up the offer. He suggested a weekend a short time ahead.

I was there all right. It was so bewilderingly attractive. I knew nothing about renovating anything, never mind a clapped-out country cottage; my limit was painting a wall and changing a fuse. At a pinch, nailing two pieces of wood together. I knew nothing about carpentry, plumbing, paving, plastering, roofing, glazing, or anything else.

This place was right out in the sticks. I did not own a car; I could not drive. The only outlet was up a steep, bramble-bowed lane leading to a lonely bus stop beside a derelict bridge. Lynton was three miles distant one way, and Barnstaple was about twenty miles the other.

It was all so – well – so *wet*. What chance did it have? For me, that is; I could not answer for the owner.

However, counsel for the defence may be able to offer just one or two points in mitigation of the rashness and soppiness of the idea.

For a start, I had once lived in just such a place. It was during the War; I had been an evacuee. I lived in a cottage, well outside a village, for eight months. A pretty primitive one at that – no gas, no electricity, no tap water, no sewerage (just a bucket out at the back). So I did know something of the nuts and bolts of basic country living.

I had the time. I was a teacher, and so in a position to do something during 'those lovely long holidays' that all non-teachers go on about.

I had the wit to realise that such an opportunity was not likely to be repeated. They say that, if God wishes to punish you, He answers your prayers – and serve you right. Well, I hadn't *prayed* for a country cottage, but I had dreamed about one, and here was God offering me one on a plate. If I passed on this, I would spend the rest of my life wondering. And God was unlikely to make a second offer to anyone so pernickety.

Finally, I had the money. Teachers are not what you might call affluent, but, even on my salary in the 1960's, I could afford two pounds a week for my 'country property', my *'pied à terre'*, my 'get-away-from-it-all' rural refuge, my chance to swank about the varied dimensions of my life.

So down I went.

*

His name was Beauchamp – Ken Beauchamp. Public-school educated, as I said – Clifton. He had clearly been associated with the area for a long time; he actually lived in a village near Bristol called Iron Acton. And, as I also said, he had been a regular Army officer – lieutenant-colonel, no less. Now he was a teacher.

Many regular soldiers (and sailors and airmen too) ended their service careers still in their forties, and a lot turned to teaching afterwards. Ken lectured, if I remember rightly, in a technical college, so he had the 'lovely long holidays' too.

He had used them to renovate rural properties. He had done it with his home at Iron Acton. He clearly had the taste for it, for no sooner had he tamed the Iron Acton house than he was on the look-out for another. He found it on a group hiking holiday in the early 1960's. It was empty, it was derelict, it seemed to have nothing to offer.

It lay beside a stream. True, one of your lovely chattering streams that the dreamers and greetings-card artists know so well, but only in the good weather. In bad weather, it can change dramatically, and fast. Curiously, it did not rush by in noisy, towering, foam-crested waves; it went brown, it went silent, and it went flat. And it was deadly.

There were streams like this all over Exmoor. In 1952, there was a wet summer, culminating in a fortnight of heavy, continuous rain. Finally, a terrible storm tipped the balance. The moor and the heather could not absorb any more water. Exmoor in effect boiled over, and all those chattering streams beloved of tourist brochures became downhill torrents, capable of sweeping away banks, trees, rocks, bridges, even rows of houses.

The worst disaster came in the town of Lynmouth, where the East and West Lyn rivers met, and wreaked havoc. At night. It must have been horrific. Twenty years later, a television crew went there to record the memories of inhabitants. Apparently nobody would talk to them, so they had to pack up and go away. The event had assumed biblical dimensions. Nearly every family lost somebody. Everybody had their story. It may have marked them, but they would not parade it for television cameras.

Ken's cottage had only been on one of the Lyn's tributaries, but it had felt the onslaught of the floods just the same. So much so that the couple who lived there at the time woke up to find it rushing past just under their bedroom window. They heard the downstairs furniture clattering up against the ceiling below. They made their escape out at the back and up the hill just in time.

By good fortune, there was a haystack in the garden at the end of the house, and it acted as a buffer against the water; otherwise the house would have gone. (A whole row of houses was swept away in a village less than a mile away downstream.) And it was a substantial house too – solid stone, built in the seventeenth century.

Understandably, the place was uninhabitable afterwards – not that it had been palatial before. There was no electricity supply. No gas, obviously. The entire water supply came through a single iron pipe and tap, which led down from a spring half-way up the hill. Toilet facilities were, presumably, buckets and cesspits. It was Ken who later installed a septic tank.

By the time Ken saw it, a decade or more later, I doubt if there was a single pane of glass in the place. Paint on woodwork must have been a mere formality. The cobbled path in the front was muffled over by half a foot of solidified residue resulting from the detritus of the flood, cattle passing and leaving their calling card, leaf mould, and general neglect. God knows what Ken saw in it.

I fancy that the owner must have been truly staggered when he was offered a price for it. But, being a Devon farmer, his instinct was

2

Arriving

One of the many colourful characters in Damon Runyon's *Guys and Dolls* – that paean to Broadway deadbeats – had occasion to recall a wry observation of his father's: 'My Daddy said to me, "Son, no madder who ya get marreed to, ya wind up marreed ta somebardy else." '

You just don't know; you have no idea what's coming. The only thing that is certain is that it won't be quite what you expected.

The same could be said, I'm sure, of parenthood, war (and peace, when it comes), constructing your first picture frame, and being president of the United States of America. It can certainly be said of house ownership – or even house tenancy – well, the sort of tenancy I was embarking upon anyway. I had never been a proprietor in my life. I had never even lived in an ordinary, three-up-and-two-down house in a road. Over the years, for a variety of inescapable circumstances, I had sojourned in upstairs lodgings, single rooms, digs, ancient college buildings, pubs, shops, army barracks and tents, and the first and second floor over a public air raid shelter.

True, my current accommodation, at last, was an honest-to-goodness flat, but all I had to do was keep it clean and give it a lick of paint now and then. The owners did all the rest – staircases, roof, courtyard, pipes, drains, and so on. I was not tempted to try and 'improve' things. I had enough sense not to tackle tasks which I knew would not turn out well. Owing to a parental separation, I had had, effectively, no father around to allow me to pick things up like that through the pores of the skin, so I was a bit short on general instinct for the subject.

So I was singularly ill-prepared for what was to come in my new 'property'. If I had had only a modicum of knowledge and general savvy, I doubt if I would have taken it on; I was insulated by my inexperience. Whatever happened was just one damn thing after another, and I did not know enough to be able to formulate a clear picture of what might follow. So I simply did the next thing, without trying to make a pattern out of it. It was a bit like Dr. Johnson's comment on a second marriage: 'The triumph of hope over experience.' Or, in my case, lack of it.

What kept me going, I suppose, was the dream. I was simply too tickled with the idea of having a 'country cottage', no matter how ignorant I was of how to develop it, or how blind I was to its short-comings, or how inadequate I was to deal with them.

It certainly didn't look much. It was low, as I said. Some of the upper rooms were constricted by sloping roofs. The lintels were also low, as I also said. No matter how hard you tried, sometimes you forgot. There was a particularly savage one leading into the hall which was capable of knocking me off my feet if I was especially preoccupied.

Downstairs floors were of concrete, naturally. Skirting boards did not exist. Paintwork was a formality. Many of the walls and beams were powdery with ancient distemper, though, to his credit, Ken had renewed many of the ceilings.

The two fireplaces in the end rooms were on the bleak side, with the very minimum of hearth or surrounding architecture to boast. The main one was, however, impressive. A mighty theatre of an opening, with that feature that estate agents are so fond of drawing your attention to, as if it were the decisive talisman which would hypnotise the prospective purchaser – a bread oven. (I never used it, and I don't think Ken ever did either.) Ken had bought an enormous backplate to the hearth (from yet another clearance sale), and installed it behind the grate, whence it did indeed throw out the heat.

It was quite a long house – five bedrooms upstairs, three very large rooms downstairs, a kitchen, and a sizeable hall. A corridor ran all the way along the back. No wonder Ken found it a little spacious for his purposes. But, for £750, who is going to turn down a cottage because it is too *big*?

Outside, at one end, was another, lower ramble of buildings, which were probably, once, shippens. Ken had turned them into a series of workshops, stores, and junk rooms. The floors were of beaten earth, as undulating as only three centuries of cattle droppings could have made them. He had run a wire out there, and the odd bare bulb dangled on scruffy flex over work benches.

Shelves were bits of splintery planks propped against bare stonework by rusty lopsided brackets. Unnamed and unnameable legions of tins, boxes, and jars perched there precariously. Only Ken would ever have known where to find anything. The nearest shippen to the house served as his garage. In the narrow gap between the house and this last shippen stood the remains of an outside toilet – presumably the only facility they had ever had, apart from the obvious chamber-pots. If you were taken short in the night at the other end of the building, it was a pretty dire trek in chilly, mud-sloshed slippers.

In view of the many stories one hears of pokey little matchboxes of rural cottages where ten children were raised in one or two bedrooms, it seems beyond argument that more than one family must have lived there.

However, it also seems certain that one part of the house had been given over to the trade, and the needs, of the main occupant. The house was called 'New Mill'.

It had one of the coolest addresses in North Devon: 'New Mill, Lynton.' It's as good as Father Christmas, isn't it? 'Santa, North Pole.'

And the 'New' was evocative. Logic dictated that, if there was a 'New' one, there must at one time have been an old one. And the *new* one went back to the late seventeenth century. Ken found a reference to it in a dusty tome in the reference section of Lynton Library – 1674, I think it was.

Several years later I came across something which has the

potential to prove the existence of that old one. I was writing an historical novel about the Domesday Book, and I used Devon as my 'background' territory. (You couldn't write a novel about the Domesday Book *everywhere*.) In the Athenaeum Library of Barnstaple, there was, and no doubt still is, a book containing not only all the Domesday entries for Devon (in Latin), but the English translation as well. It must of course all be digitised by now.

Naturally I was interested in the entries for the area around 'New Mill, Lynton'. One of the local Norman feudal tenants was a man called William Capra, and it recorded that in one of the manors which he held – the manor of 'Lyn' – there was a *'novum molendinum'*. A 'new mill', no less.

Now that does not, of course, prove that Capra's mill was the predecessor of my 'New Mill' (or rather Ken's 'New Mill'). But it is odd, to say the least. The population of eleventh-century Devon was not high, and it could be argued that the 'manor of Lyn' would have been unlikely to need two mills. On the other hand, I doubt if the boundaries of Capra's manor of Lyn could be drawn with total accuracy today, so we don't know for sure where his mill was.

But, at the very least, it makes you think, and gives you a ghostly sense of contact with the deep past. If it wasn't our mill, there was most certainly a mill around here, and in 1086 (the year of Domesday Book) it was a 'new' one, and that in itself provides a distinct *frisson*. Had there been an 'old' mill in 1086? Was a miller plying his trade near our great sycamore, with the tiny waterfall at its foot, nine centuries ago? I found New Mill in 1967, and the Conquest happened in 1066. Nine hundred and one years ago.

We also know what powered our mill. Water.

Here you open up a vast, complicated, and, if you are so disposed, absorbing, topic. The whole business of discovering and harnessing the power of water and wind (and tide) gives the lie to the idea that medieval technology was backward and primitive. There was a great deal more to rural life in the Middle Ages than what we learned in our primary school projects about 'a typical village', with its strips and its ploughteams.

For instance, we have evidence of ancient Greek and Roman writers discussing water mills long before the Middle Ages even began. One of them, Vitruvius, produced a set of instructions for constructing one. They had also tumbled to the idea in ancient China, but then the Chinese tumbled to most things very early, didn't they? Archaeologists are still pondering the implication of discoveries in silt deposits in northern Europe from the first century AD, well away from the 'culture' of Rome.

Between them all, they had worked out the respective merits of vertical wheels and horizontal wheels, and had tackled the problem of gears to transfer the power of a vertical wheel to a horizontal millstone. Mills were being built not only to assist the production of flour but textiles, paper, lumber, and metals.

Windmills admittedly seem to have come later, perhaps in regions where rivers were too sluggish to drive anything very much. Why were they sluggish? Often because the land was flat. If the land was flat it was more likely to be swept by wind. Work it out for yourself. It can surely be no coincidence that so many Dutch land-scape paintings feature windmills.

Windmills were, if not numerous, commonplace by the twelfth century. Though they were vastly outnumbered by water-mills. (Curious how we put the hyphen in 'water-mill' but leave it out in 'windmill'.)

In Norman England there were water-mills all over the place. And one of them was very likely at the foot of a hill in the 'manor of Lyn', according to Domesday Book. Along the foot of the hill behind the house, there was a long ledge, which was clearly the mill leet – the tiny stream which powered the mill, which made the flanges move and the great wheel turn.

There were two types of water wheel. (As you can see, these discoveries prompted some research on the part of both Ken and me, so I am a small mine of information on the subject.) Depending on natural local topography, the water of the leet reached the wheel at its top or its bottom. So you had an overshot wheel or an undershot wheel. Either way the water hit each flange and pushed it several degrees in its circle. The combined weight of each flange, and the water it harboured, together of course with gravity as each flange descended with its own weight, turned the great wheel, while the now-empty flanges were raised on the opposite side of the wheel, to the top, where it all happened again. For ever, if necessary. In practice, of course, the miller had a set of sluices which enabled him to control the head of water from the leet. The water which was not needed was allowed to run off, which it did at the foot of the sycamore. A sycamore then in illustrious company – a mill leet near the left base, a waterfall near the right base, and, all round, a mass of vigorous, nodding primroses, which, whipped by the spatters of the water, constantly leapt like a flower bed with St. Vitus' Dance. It was a sight you never tired of looking at.

The next-to-end wall showed the marks where the wheel had been set, though of course the wheel itself had long gone. The roof had long gone too, and there was no way of knowing whether there had been one storey or two. Almost certainly this structure had housed the mill machinery – the business part. Ken had found a piece of masonry which arguably was part of a millstone, but we never took steps to prove it.

Looking at the cobbles of the frontage, and the awful stones in the path leading down from the road – and the steepness of it – one's heart went out to the browbeaten oxen who had had to stagger and struggle, dragging the sacks of freshly-cut corn, or freshly-ground flour – straining to stop their solid-wheel carts pulling them back on the way up and running away with them on the way down.

All that sweat and effort; all the whipping and driving; all the cloven hoofs sliding and scrabbling desperately to gain a foothold on wet stones and rutted mud; all the terrible weights; all the remorseless toil. For so many centuries. And buildings like this are now sought-after as romantic rural hideaways, and described by their city visitors as 'idyllic' and 'quaint'.

Neither Ken nor I regarded New Mill as 'romantic' or 'idyllic'. Or 'quaint'. True, it didn't inflict medieval suffering, and we had a choice about being there. But we were under no illusions about it.

So many people who have never lived in the country think that it is so desirable. All that space, and fresh air, and healthy glow on cheeks, Well, yes. But life anywhere is complicated, and just as full of problems as anywhere else. Wherever you are, you have to make the drains work; you have to see that the switches are efficient; you have to keep the garden under control; you have to stock the larder; you have to pay the bills.

If public facilities are rarer, and distances longer, and shops further away, and public transport more occasional. . . well, it doesn't help. Put simply, life in New Mill wasn't easy. It raised your respect for all those rustic families who had had to survive in houses like it.

But it did have its moments. The waterfall I have just described was one of them. I never would have foreseen it, but I developed the habit of taking a shower under it first thing in the morning. That wasn't idyllic or quaint either, but it was undeniably bracing. It required much resolve to get under it. However, you staggered out afterwards it with much pride, satisfaction, smugness – and of course relief. I should think those Indian fakirs needed just as much determination when they did their morning promenade over the bed of hot coals which is an inescapable feature of the well-run household of every Indian fakir. But they were great seekers after virtue, and no doubt they felt their immortal souls blooming beneath the burden of pain and hardship and blistered soles. Well, I used to feel a bit like that.

Then there was all that stuff *growing* everywhere. Some of it of course, you could do without – like the Russian rhubarb which threatened to take over the far bank of the stream, and the Japanese knotweed, which was engaged in creeping dominion of the area behind the house, between the kitchen and the leet. Nettles and brambles, naturally. Life was a running battle between the occupier and the edges and hedges which, if not continually fought against, could advance to take over completely.

But that was not the whole picture. Flowers were abundant – snowdrops, primroses, wild violets, daffodils, bluebells. Later on a touch of lilac, hawthorn, foxglove, campion, speedwell, cowslip, herb robert, wild garlic, rose bay willow herb. A few dog-roses. Millions of daisies and buttercups. And an unaccountable grove of raspberry canes.

Round the front door (well, one of the front doors – Ken had the idea of turning it into two dwellings; that was why I was there) was a large climber with red flowers – japonica.

Only we called it 'the japonical'.

In the early days, Ken had imported a handyman from his other house at Iron Acton, to do various maintenance and construction jobs that were within the scope of a knowledgeable pensioner. His name was Mr. Bousher, and he was a Bristol man.

It may be common knowledge, but it was hitherto unknown to me, that the Bristol accent had a habit of sticking the letter 'l' at the end of a lot of words that ended in a vowel. So Mr. Bousher promptly christened the front door climber the 'japonical'. Ken told me, and together, out of amused respect for Mr. Bousher, we thereafter regularly followed suit.

Ken would regale me with other epithets Mr. Bousher had come out with. 'Fuchsials' is one I remember from quite early on. (North Devon is in fact very good 'fuchsial' country.) Ken's favourite was Mr. Bousher's verdict on a sagging beam: 'What you need here is a steel girdle.'

Not content with that, we went on to invent other Bousherisms, whenever the opportunity presented itself. One evocative term was the name for a seriously upset stomach: 'Diarrhoeal.'

Fuchsial, japonical, girdle, diarrhoeal – they all passed into New Mill vernacular.

New Mill, as I hope I have explained, was on the floor of a valley. Behind the house rose a hillside. At one end of the house the lane rose to the old bridge beside the road, about three or four hundred yards, I suppose. Across the river from front of the house there was a field, beyond which another hillside rose. And away to the right, at the other end of the house, another field led, between hills, to our only neighbour, about another four hundred yards away.

The hills were indeed a disadvantage. It meant that the hours of sunshine were restricted. It was light, but it was not bright. Well, not for long.

So that was a pity. But you had peace; you had quiet; you had privacy. I had no worries about an audience for my morning shower. The path down the lane and past the house was a public right of way, but walkers were far from numerous. One shook one's head at the city girls who tripped past in skimpy skirts and high heels. One passed the time of day with farmers going about their business. One thanked the postman who actually walked all the way down from the road to deliver a circular or a bill. And one fumed in impotence at the noisy crowd of hunt followers who surged past with total disregard for anything other than the chase. But such intrusions were not frequent.

You relied by and large on your own company. (No telephone, I forgot to say. And no telly.)

But you were never completely alone; the stream chattered away day and night.

3

Starting

Was Ken going to get value for his two pounds a week?

I knew nothing about country cottages, apart from a lonely sojourn in one as a seven-year-old evacuee. I wasn't very happy there; I was the only child in four who did not belong to the family, and I soon became the rear-end Charlie when it came to handing out favours. The wonder is that I developed this fondness for 'the country' – or at any rate for Devon – in spite of the deprivations of parent and home, in spite of occasional bullying at school (the locals naturally took it out on 'London kids'), and in spite of an appreciable level of general neglect by the women of the house.

I quite liked the village school; I enjoyed the three-quarter-mile walk each way, between banks and hedges full of primroses and violets and cow parsley and foxgloves and campion and all the rest. My teacher introduced me to Kenneth Grahame's *Wind in the Willows*, and from the start of it I was hooked. Even at seven I became aware of a totally wistful, if impractical, resolve that one day I would like to live 'in the country'.

That was all very well. Now, here I was. I wasn't going to get very far with cosy impressions of wild violets and Ratty's adventures with Mole. As I said, I could swing a paint-brush, and put up a shelf at a pinch (oh, yes, and I had laid a carpet or two). But that was about it. All I had to offer was keenness, good health, and time (twelve or thirteen weeks a year).

I didn't know Ken from Adam. Was he going to be efficient or a bumbler? Did he have any overall plan, any timetable (however vague)? Did he really have any idea how long it was all going to take?

Did he have the funds to see it through? I didn't know about renovation, but I did know that it cost money. Had I taken on something completely beyond me?

By the same token Ken had invited a completely unknown quantity to share his house, albeit as separate dwellings. (It occurs to me now – though it did not occur then – that this arrangement might seem a touch suggestive. But let me hasten to assure the reader – particularly the prudish reader, or the prurient reader – that there was no other dimension to the association. And in the next few years we both took wives.) How were two strangers going to work together, and one of them an ignoramus? Was Ken going to get his money's worth?

He certainly got the time. I soon learned that he kept long hours. Since the deal was that I should help him, it seemed incumbent upon me to try and keep pace with him. The working day did not end at five, or six, or even, sometimes, seven. This applied especially in the summer, because of the longer evenings of daylight.

He seemed quite tireless. He had no air of bustle about him, and you rarely saw him dishevelled with effort, but he could keep going in his deliberate, persistent way for hours. And he was twenty years older than I was, as I later discovered. In fact, there was one holiday when I had to come home early (I forget why), and I was so exhausted with the cumulative effect of a fortnight's effort, that I sat in my flat for the whole of the following day. And I mean 'sat'. I simply sat down and gazed at nothing in particular. Hour after hour. I must have had meals, but my abiding memory of that day is sitting. No reading, no working, no telly, nothing – just sitting.

He used to hum to himself. Endlessly. I don't think he knew he was doing it. It was interrupted only if he came to a particular point in the work which involved especial effort, strain, stretching, or concentration – say, with electrical jobs or lofty beams. One tune he was fond of (his tastes were classical rather than popular) was the Pilgrims' Chorus from *Tannhäuser*. So the accompaniment to installation of, say, a switch mechanism or a brick in an awkward place went something like this: 'Dah-daah. . . . dah-daaah, da-da-da.

. . . dah-dah-da. . . . daah-dah-da. . . . daaaaah-dah. . . . dah'. And so on. It was amazing that he never lost the tune; he never missed a beat. But the spaces drove you crazy as you waited for him to drop the other shoe.

Crazy or not, I learnt about – or at least became acquainted with – installing wash-basins. Or rather I did the heavy bit, holding them in place while Ken got to work with the nuts and plugs and plumber's spanners. Ken insisted on calling them 'wash-basins', I had always referred to them as 'sinks', but he smugly pointed out that the one referred to bathrooms and bedrooms and the other referred to kitchens and sculleries. He used to tease me by saying that if you came from a public school you said 'wash-basin', but if you came from a grammar school, or, worse, a council school, you said 'sink'. (It's rather like the debate over the downstairs room in which you spent most of your leisure time: was it a 'lounge', a 'drawing room', a 'sitting room', or a 'parlour'? And what level of society was implied by the use of each one? I'm sure whole books have been written about this. I know at least one was; the whole nation had a spell when it debated what was 'U' and 'non-U'.)

Ken was, as I said, public school – Clifton. And it showed. His diction was cut-glass. His manners were very correct. On the face of it, he was what one meant by the phrase 'perfect gentleman'. Everything, like his manners, was correct. No saint, mark you. And he told a passable dirty story. (But then most ex-public schoolboys of my experience can do that in their sleep.)

He had a divorce behind him, but I had no evidence on the rights and wrongs of the case. All I knew was that her name was Martha. He referred to her only to tell me about the divorce. I never met her. There were two children – grown up now. The daughter was married; I forget her Christian name. She and her husband visited from time to time, but they kept well separate from my half of the house. I met the son, Julian, only once or twice. He sold advertising space for television.

Ken had spent most of his professional life in the Army. Royal Army Service Corps – hence the endless practical knowledge he displayed about the house. He had made it to Lieutenant-Colonel. I don't know whether he was Sandhurst-trained, or whether he had, like so many young men in 1939, simply joined up, and won his promotion on merit as the War developed. After hostilities were over, perhaps he stayed on, again like many ex-soldiers, because he had found the life to his taste; because it had become the only life he knew as an adult; or because, as an officer, that life was a rather good one. At any rate, he was used to technical matters and authority. So it was a natural progression, when he retired, that he should lecture at a technical college. Bristol, for all I know.

He was one of those people who were perpetually attracted to things mechanical. He owned at least two cars, one of them a vintage Wolseley – open-top – which he brought down the hill sometimes – and got it up again, very loudly. A maroon beast, with tubes and brass and chrome and pipes all over the place. When he wasn't involved in jobs about the house, he was in the 'garage' (well, the old shippen) tinkering with something or other.

When he wasn't tinkering with New Mill or with the Wolseley, he was tinkering with his other house at Iron Acton. I don't think it bothered him that none of these projects ever showed the slightest sign of nearing completion. As with the explorer and the long-distance traveller, the journey was much more important and satisfying than the arrival.

For this reason, the expedient was much more attractive than the ultimate solution. If anything broke, stopped, burst, played up, slowed down, coughed, choked, or got bunged up (New Mill rather lent itself to behaviour like this), he would cobble something together to provide what was obviously a temporary solution, but this temporary solution showed a consistent tendency to stay around long after its original planned period of usefulness. I used to joke that the whole place was held together with pink binder twine. Not true, of course, but it made a good story, and it did give the taste of the place.

Take Mole's Chamber.

Outside one of the kitchens (there were two dwellings,

remember) Ken had installed a catchment tank to take the waste from the kitchen sink (not the kitchen 'wash basin' but the kitchen 'sink'). The trouble was that there was no natural soak-away, because gravity was against it. By this time a septic tank had been installed, so it was a simple matter of getting the kitchen waste from the catchment tank to the septic tank.

The trouble was, as I have already explained, that New Mill was built into the side of a hill, and the ground rose sharply behind the kitchen at the back. The main pipe leading from the toilet to the septic tank was higher than the kitchen catchment tank. No problem at all. Ken installed a pump under its manhole cover. There was some kind of trigger device which set off an electric pump when the waste reached a certain level.

That sounds efficient enough, but the pump was not always to be relied upon. Moreover, much of the kitchen waste was greasy, from all the washing up. When it got cold, the result can easily be imagined. If ever you were sated with lovely views and shy violets and nodding foxgloves and tinkling streams, all you had to do was lift the manhole cover and feast your eyes on the unspeakable sight underneath.

What has all this got to do with moles? Because one of the topographical features of Exmoor was the spot where Farmer Mole – so the story went – went riding back one night to his farm from the pub. It was late, it was dark, it was raining cats and dogs, and there was a notorious bog near the path he proposed to take. He had probably had a jar of cider too many, but he pooh-poohed his friends' advice to stay indoors, or at least to go home another way. You can work it out for yourself. The rain, the dark, the cider, the bravado ('I know this path like the back of my hand, and I'm not as drunk as some thinkle peep'): neither Farmer Mole nor his horse were ever seen again.

The place shows up on the Ordnance Survey map as 'Mole's Chamber'. So here was a ready-made name for our kitchen catchment tank. Apt: the one was as noisome as the other.

After the mini-sagas of the sinks (sorry – wash-basins), I later became a witness to the installation of the toilet facilities. Even Ken – binder twine or no binder twine – recognised that the time would come when something better than an Elsan would have to be provided. Especially if he wanted female visitors – and he was quite partial to female visitors. He had a trick of attracting female company, and it was difficult to see how he did it. Tallish, beaky nose, very spare physique, glasses, baggy shorts – well, you see what I mean.

Incidentally, this went on, long after we had left New Mill. He used to pay us an occasional visit well into his seventies, maybe even later. (He was divorced again by this time.) And he was never short of the company of a lady. And I stress 'lady'. They really were. Just what was his secret?

Anyway, the Elsan. In order to save money, Ken had utilised the long corridor which ran the length of the first storey at the back of the house. He put in two partitions, and a door in each one. The Elsan went in between, and there was a catch on each door. That sounded fine, but it did not take note of human behaviour.

Ideally, the doors had of course to be lockable, and unlockable, from each side. If the inhabitant from side A wanted to make sure of privacy, he (or she) would naturally lock the side B door. The trouble was that he would forget to unlock it when he (or she) left, and the next customer from the other side was locked out. So the only solution was to have a catch on either side instead of a lock.

That meant that anybody had access from either side at any time. One way to avoid embarrassment was to make a noise when you were approaching, so that any previous arrival had time to shout a warning. Luckily the bare boards of the corridors helped in this. But inevitably there were the sort of incidents one could easily imagine.

This arrangement went on long after he had installed a flush toilet there, because the geography of the house stayed the same.

Curiously, Ken took much more care with the washing and bathing amenities than he did with the toilets. Although, on consideration, perhaps not so curiously. I don't know what you would have done, but, after my experience in New Mill, I tended to revise my priorities. Ken, I thought, was right about his wash-basins (and, later, his bath). Which was the more important? Which would you prefer: an Elsan, and H. and C. in bath and wash-basin, or a shiny flush toilet and a large china bowl and water jug on the sideboard?

Speaking as a historian, I should say it is an indisputable fact that the arrival of clean, piped water to the house in the nineteenth century had a far greater effect on human welfare than the installation of the water-closet in the eighteenth. In fact, the disposal of the effluent from these water-closets, in London at any rate, proved catastrophic; it was piped away into the Thames, whence the city drew its drinking water. The cholera epidemics in the first half of the nineteenth century were not coincidence or bad luck or the wrath of God.

Which brings me inexorably to the business of the septic tank.

Clearly, if we were going to have a flush toilet installed – and a bath for that matter – we were going to need a means of disposing of the effluent from them. We were miles from mains sewerage. So it would have to be a septic tank.

Septic tanks were a new world to me. I was like nearly everybody else; I just pulled the chain and left. Where it all went was not a mystery; it was a non-event. My command of such matters was about the same as that of the city child who thought that milk came out of a bottle, not a cow.

I soon learned. Before long I was fluent in terms like tip trays, filter beds, gravitational fall, and soak-aways. I found out that lady guests had to be taken on one side, and, very diplomatically, informed that they could not dispose of tampons down the pan. The only things that could go down was toilet paper and – well, you know. The filter bed could not cope with anything else.

The whole unit was installed over a boiling hot Easter weekend. Can you remember *any* Easter weekend when it was boiling hot? Well, this one was. I have rarely worked so hard. Ken had previously had two huge holes dug – mechanically – one for the filter bed and one for the tank itself. So all we had to do was line them with breeze blocks, I think it was.

Not even Ken's wide technical experience enabled him to cope with this on his own (I was no use except to fetch and carry). And he knew that there was no way he could hold a filter bed together with binder twine. So he hired a local mason. (Name of David Crocombe. More of him later.) Devon is very good at masons – all that stone everywhere. The garden at New Mill was chock full of them – though I suspect that many of them were the remains of broken walls and pathways, buried under the weight of long neglect and overgrowth after the flood. A bit like Pompeii under the layer of ash from Vesuvius.

And those masons were – are – very good at walls. If you want a good wall built, get hold of a few tons of stone from a Devon quarry and hire a Devon mason – and stand back.

Building a filter bed and a septic tank was routine to David, almost to the point of being automatic, but it was fascinating to watch him at work – steady, deliberate, unhurried – and it grew almost by magic. All the time, he therefore had the mental energy to keep one entertained with a constant stream of anecdote, which, as he neared the climax of a particular story, caused his voice to rise almost in octaves of incredulity.

I learned just a little of the chemistry of septic tanks – how they never completely filled up, how chemicals broke down the effluent, how the top of it formed a crust. And the soak-away really did soak away. Of course it did need draining by mechanical means from time to time, but such was the effectiveness of these chemicals (and the mysterious filter bed – just what did that do?), it was a matter of years rather than months – depending of course on the number of people in the house. Ken and I were only there in the holidays, so the system was never under any strain.

This may not strike an informed reader as a particularly coherent account, much less a knowledgeable one. I'm sorry about that. But you were always learning with septic tanks. When I moved to a proper house in another part of Devon, I found that that it too depended on a septic tank. One day there was a blockage around the pipes draining off the last effluent into the soak-away, and this man, in order to repair it, actually descended into the tank itself. Put on oilskins or whatever it is they use, and went right down, so that you couldn't see his head. *Into a septic tank.* And he was a big man. Routine apparently.

The country teaches you, among things, that proximity to dirt is not automatically or necessarily unhealthy. The water supply to the house – we are back at New Mill now – had originally been one cast-iron pipe from a nearby spring a quarter of the way up the hill.

Even Ken thought that was a bit much, and he did a good job of installing lots of plastic pipes to take the water to his wash-basins and baths and toilets (and sinks in the kitchens – two dwellings, remember). Taps and plugs and ballcocks all over the place. But the water still had to come from the spring up the hill. So he put in a long (a very long) black plastic pipe. I later discovered that it actually drew the supply from a tiny little stream running from the spring, which was regularly crossed and re-crossed by cattle with, potentially, diseases like liver-fluke. This fed into a catchment tank (made of asbestos!), which gradually produced enough head of water to drive the water down to the house.

Spring water oozing from the grass, cow pats, liver fluke, more catchment tanks, asbestos, and miles of plastic pipe through the bracken – an inspector today would have a fit. But I later acquired a wife and stepsons, and later still another son of my own, and we raised them all there for five years. And none of them was ever ill.

Perhaps the trick was that one should never look for, or aspire to, perfection. Just make it work. Make it liveable in. Pay attention to the nuts and bolts, the buttons and the stitches – all the unromantic things which we do not like to have to consider, never mind attend to, but without which a house like New Mill could not function.

I work currently as a school archivist, in an independent, part-boarding school on the edge of Exmoor, right out in Injun country. I have often had reason, naturally, to consult the minutes of governors' meetings. And what does one find? Not dramatic episodes, great crises, epic struggles, staff vendettas, sensitive scandals, esoteric discussion of educational philosophy, no. The most frequent topics one comes across are matter-of-fact items about drains, coal supplies, oil lamps, outside toilets, cesspits, and outbreaks of infectious disease.

By the same token, the history of New Mill in the time I was there – and it was eight years in all – was not about fragrant honeysuckle up the wall, and sultry afternoons in deckchairs, and gazing fondly on lambs gambolling in distant fields, and leisurely hours picking fruit from the raspberry canes at the foot of the hill; it was about dirt and mice and mud and mild flooding, about smoking fireplaces, about colonies of ants going up the wall, about ancient grinding door locks. Put another way, it was about filter beds and Mole's Chamber.

4

Learning

However, for the first two years or so, filter beds and Mole's Chamber were barely more than a gleam in Ken Beauchamp's eyes. I was able to go there only in school holidays – mostly a week or ten days at a time. Each visit, then, was a novelty, an adventure, a change, an escape – which was looked forward to as a regular treat. It was just as a small boy used to look forward to the seaside; he was not put off by crowds, early rising, packed train compartments, railways snacks, suitcases, trudging three quarters of a mile to poky digs. (All that of course dates me pretty ruthlessly. But one could just as easily today cite in their place overheated and overcrowded cars, airport queues, flight delays, traffic jams, and travel sickness.)

What mattered to that boy was the sand, the ice cream, the freedom, the late nights, the endless fish and chips, fry-ups, and baked beans. So it was with me; what mattered was the peace, the freedom, the open fires, the river, the leisure. The Elsan and the low lintels were all a totally acceptable part of the picture. The important thing was that it was all mine. Well, Ken's, but I was the legal tenant, and I was quite often there when Ken was at Iron Acton, knocking his other house into shape. So I could feel, almost behave, as if it were mine.

Subconsciously I knew that, before very long, I could go back to relax in the carpeted comfort of a tame, warm flat, raid the fridge, and turn on the telly whenever I wanted.

But it was interesting that, come the holidays, I began to think of New Mill not only as the best place to go to, but as the *only* place to go to. I never felt in any way constricted about this. It simply didn't occur to me to go anywhere else.

It would have been enough to make eight out of ten other people cringe – the quarter-mile steeply-descending path, the slippery and jutting rocks in it, the overgrowth as well as the undergrowth, the fading paintwork, the chill when you opened the door after several weeks of absence and emptiness (and remember it was a stone house). Everything had to be started up from scratch. Switches had to be turned on and fuses checked; logs had to be sawn and brought in; the paraffin heater (one of my first purchases) had to be set going; the Elsan had to be 'charged' ready for use.

Then there was the small question of food. I had no car; even if I had, I would have hesitated to bring it down New Mill Lane, for the simple reason that I was not confident that I would be able to get it back up again. It really was very steep, with a couple of savage bends. So I had not been able to bring boxes of provisions, overloading the boot and bulging the back seat with vital food – and drink. Everything I wanted to bring with me had to go into a rucksack. The nearest village was Barbrook, about a mile and a half away.

Luckily they had a post office and general store there. As soon as the vital procedures were up and running, there was nothing for it but rucksack and hike.

It was here that I received my first favour. Have you noticed, whenever you declare your intention to embark on something unorthodox, you are never short of people to tell you that it is ill-considered, insufficiently thought out, impractical, poorly resourced, or just plain daft? But when you have actually embarked, when you have actually shoved off, and you show that you mean business, sooner or later you will meet people who offer sound advice or practical help. Very often sooner.

While I was standing in the Barbrook General Stores and Post Office, and looking at my rucksack, and deciding whether, in the interests of weight or space, I should leave out the baked beans or the streaky bacon, the proprietor, a cheery soul called Stan Marsh, offered the welcome information that 'we deliver, you know'.

And he did. No charge. Stan Marsh was my third acquaintance in North Devon. The tea man was the first. I discovered that he ran a little complex of holiday bungalows or flats on the road between Barbrook and New Mill. So Mr. Meddick (I never found out what his Christian name was) introduced me to North Devon. Stan Marsh gave me the means of feeding myself without having to walk a mile and half each way to obtain anything from a bar of soap to a bottle of milk. And Ken Beauchamp, of course, was putting a roof over my head.

You see? They were all doing me a favour in one way or another. If I had sat down first and drawn up lists of vital food items or affordable rents or rentable properties in the area, I should never have got going. It is a good argument for the idea that, if you are faced with a daunting prospect, the best way to start is to start, and it matters little where.

Stan Marsh went further. He said that if, before my next visit, I phoned him to say what I would like in the way of immediate supplies, he would have a box of them ready for me at the top of New Mill Lane by the railway bridge. (Not even Stan Marsh's kindness stretched to bringing his van down the lane, and I don't blame him.)

So I quickly fell into a regular sequence, every bit of which was enjoyable. Up at crack of dawn, pack the rucksack with a fresh set of necessities (and a few luxuries, which grew in number with the passing months), up to London, and catch the eight o'clock train from Paddington to Exeter.

There was always a restaurant car on this train. And I mean a proper restaurant car, not a bar counter where you were sold unopenable plastic packets of fruit cake or coffee in flimsy cups with slivers of plywood to stir the sugar secreted in narrow little tubes of paper. Nor do I mean a first-class carriage where they would bring a bacon sandwich to your seat.

No. I mean a full soup-and-fish restaurant car (open to everybody, not just the nobs) with tablecloths and napkins and little lights that made you look so superior to humble mortals on station plat-forms as you slid past. Well, not a soup-and-fish dinner, but a full bacon-and-egg breakfast, hot and fresh, served by waiters in white monkey jackets, men of fathomless experience, poise, and resource, who could, on a moving train, swing a coffee pot across the table and fill your cup to the millilitre without spilling a drop. And not just egg and bacon; tomatoes, mushrooms, stacks of slices of bread and butter, and toast *ad lib* (marmalade of course), and coffee till it trickled out of the top of your head. Oh – and sauté potatoes – an absolute delight.

Nobody rushed you. If you wanted to spin it out, you could fill a good hour and be halfway to Exeter by the time you had finished. And for this, what did we pay? Wait for it – 67½p. Thirteen shillings and sixpence. A tip for the waiter and you were still within shouting distance of three-quarters of a pound.

And this wasn't the Middle Ages; it wasn't George Stephenson; it was 1967.

At Exeter I caught the 'country crawler' up to Barnstaple. A few years before I began my trips to North Devon, there had been not one line to Barnstaple, but two – one up from Exeter, and one from Taunton direct to Barnstaple. It neatly avoided the great dog's leg down to Exeter and back up again. It trundled through places like Norton Fitzwarren, Wiveliscombe, Bampton, East Anstey, Swimbridge, and Landkey. Now the stations are all gone. The victims either of Dr. Beeching or of later 'economy cuts'.

This is not strictly relevant, but I can't see when I shall ever get another opportunity to get it in. In the previous decade, I had once had occasion to travel to Gloucestershire, to the town of Winchcombe – well, to the station nearest to it, about a mile away. You couldn't get there in one go; the Olympian planners in London terminals had probably never heard of places like Winchcombe. But they did direct you to a place where you could change trains to get there. They had gleaned a rumour in a trainspotter's guide that there was a branch line.

It's rather like Columbus' advisers and backers. 'Quite simple: go to Lisbon and hire a boat to take you to Cathay. Go west. From then on you're on your own. But you can't miss it.'

Well, this wasn't Lisbon; it was Honeybourne Junction. I can't think of a lovelier name for a country railway station. And it was all there (this is a shameless nostalgia jag) – somnolent platforms, green cardboard return tickets that you tore in half, porters with peaked caps and tiny black waistcoats; waiting rooms with fireplaces; milk churns waiting to be picked up; great wooden barrows with enormously long arms; and the well-tended, eye-melting flower-beds.

There must have been hundreds, maybe thousands, of Honeybourne Junctions all over the country, and most of them were sacrificed on the altar of cost-effectiveness. Well, I hope their gods of stern economy were satisfied, but one's heart goes out to the benign deities of sentiment, fondness, familiarity, and comfort, who didn't want anything sacrificed at all, and would have been content with mere loyalty.

So I soldiered on down to Exeter and caught the crawler to Barnstaple. That line, mercifully, has bucked the trend. It has survived. So here you pass through stations with similarly evocative names like Newton St. Cyres, Yeoford, Copplestone, Eggesford, Portsmouth Arms, King's Nympton, and Umberleigh, on the way to the terminus at Barnstaple (which once upon a time had hosted not one station, but four).

It has had a charmed life over the years I have known it. Many a rumour has rumbled round the county about the Damocles sword of closure hanging over it. But it has contradicted them all – partly, one suspects, because the authorities have decided that it is good for tourism, and where would Devon be without tourism? Renaming it the 'Tarka Line' (after Henry Williamson's classic book about a Devon otter) has no doubt played a part. Like Robert Louis Stevenson: he couldn't sell a novel entitled *The Sea Cook*, but as soon as he renamed it *Treasure Island*, he had no trouble.

So – Barnstaple. But that was only the third quarter of the journey. The next, and last stage, was the Lynton bus, the 310 – a single-storey green chugger which plied its way through places like Bratton Fleming, Blackmoor Gate, Parracombe, Woody Bay, and, finally, down a precipitous hill, to Lynton.

For all that this was a quiet rural route, things happened on it that would never be seen in a city. One day, as we were passing between two hedges which were slightly lower than the traditional Devon high ones, the driver caught sight of something that had escaped the notice of the passengers, who, because this was a regular run for them, were not taking much notice of anything. He suddenly pulled up, got out, crossed the road, opened a gate, and went up into the field behind it. Our eyes followed him as he approached a sheep on its back. The vainly jerking legs told the tale. He bent down, grabbed the fleece with the ease of much practice, and hauled it to its feet. Rubbing his hands on bunches of grass to get rid of the surplus grease and dirt, he came back, carefully shut the gate, crossed the road again, and climbed back into his seat. He was met with a round of applause.

My stop was a cross-roads, Caffyn's Cross, beside, as I said, a derelict railway bridge. The bridge had belonged to yet another railway line, the narrow-gauge between Lynton and Barnstaple (closed in 1935 – yet another one-time terminus in Barnstaple).

Then it was humping the rucksack, stopping to see if Stan Marsh had left his packet of provisions as promised (and he had), and beginning the descent of New Mill Lane. The engine of the bus faded into the distance towards Barbrook, and I used to stop, between the brambles and the campion and the wild garlic. And I would listen. Nothing.

Then on to the rusty lock, the damp air, and the cold stone behind the grit-grinding front door.

*

I surprised myself with the ease with which I evolved a routine. I suppose being a committee of one helped. These were bachelor days – well, to begin with anyway. Then, too, this was probably the first time in my life when I could organise a week or a fortnight without being beholden to anybody (that is, when Ken was not there).

I was on holiday – part of those 'lovely long holidays' people went on about. The pay-cheque was coming in, albeit a modest assistant teacher's salary. But even I could afford £2 a week, and I was eating no more than I would have done in my flat at home.

There was no problem about rising. For a start I had not gone to bed late. There was no telly and no radio. I simply packed up when I was tired of reading in front of the fire. I had the company of the river to see me off at night and to wake me up the next day. Even more so in summer, when you could keep the bedroom window open. With no alarm clock I was waking up at six-thirty, six o'clock, even, memorably, half-past five once or twice. And not just waking up; ready to go.

If weather permitted, there was the shower beneath the sycamore, with, admittedly, a fair amount of teeth-grinding. Again, if the temperature permitted, breakfast would be taken sitting on the doorstep – cereal, boiled eggs, toast and marmalade. None of your standing gulp and dash, eyes watering and cheeks bulging with damp cornflakes. (I must explain that, though we had few of the common utilities, we did have gas, albeit in cylinders – which all of course had to be lugged down the hill.)

In the morning there were the chores to do – washing up (and no dish-washer), plain washing, ironing (Ken had installed electricity by the time I arrived), humping in logs for the evening fire, carrying on with whatever project Ken had begun – like sanding old whitewash off beams, bringing some kind of order to the chaos of stones at the edge of the river (endlessly absorbing; anything to do with water always is; you had to keep an eye on the clock).

In fact you had to keep an eye on the clock all the time. Morning *and* afternoon. *Everything* you tackled could become absorbing. Rather like looking up a film star in an encyclopaedia; you became so side-tracked by names you had not thought about for years that you forgot who it was you had been been looking up in the first place. Never more than a couple of hours on anything – stone-moving, log-stacking, carpentry, furniture-rearranging, cooking, You had to get used to leaving jobs incomplete, promising yourself that you would come back to them tomorrow. If you didn't, you could find a pile of untended laundry, a grate empty of fuel, and an evening meal still waiting to be cooked at eight o'clock.

You saw people too – the new owner of the stables and guesthouse up the valley, the farmer up at the top of New Mill Lane, Joe Pyall the postman, who toiled right down the hill to bring the post, the retired lady who regularly brought her Labrador dog down to the river for his exercise walk. People have to be talked to. But you didn't always know when they were coming. Difficult to plan for. Flexibility was all.

And dammit, I had gone there, among other things, to relax. I liked reading, and I fancied myself as a writer. What was the point of going to all that trouble, travelling and spending all that time and money, simply in order to keep everything at bay?

I enjoyed everything I was doing, but I had to arrange the day so that I could relax, read, and write. So it was a mental exercise as well as a physical one, and you derived a great deal of satisfaction at whatever measure of success you achieved in either. And you learned not to be annoyed, frustrated, or disappointed at not meeting whatever targets you might set yourself.

True, it could rain, sometimes quite a lot. But there were always a dozen things waiting to be seen to indoors. There was always the log fire (which, with its obstinate habit of smoking when you least wanted it to, was a separate project in itself).

There was the bus to Lynton and Barnstaple if you wanted a day out. (And it usually did take most of the day. Devon country buses were not like London tube trains.) Ordinary shops in streets took on much more attractiveness when you spent most of your day alone in a remote cottage, however enjoyable that practice may have been.

But, when the weather was benign enough to go out, you did. Devon is an 'out' place. In one freak spell of mild weather, I once took my lunch outside on Boxing Day. It could often be what the holiday promoters said about the East Anglian coast – 'bracing' – but you usually felt much fitter by the time you went back.

There may too have been a subconscious factor in all this. I had been evacuated in the War, as I said, and I had spent eight months in a Devon cottage just as remote as mine, and with even fewer facilities – no electricity, no gas cylinders, no running water (a hand pump at the bottom of the field), not even an Elsan (just a bucket out at the back).

At the age of seven you don't take a great deal of notice of this; life is a matter of being told get up, get dressed, sit up at the table, go to school, behave yourself, and there isn't any more jam for a sandwich (rationing). Well, it was for me; I was an evacuee – no family, no mates, no neighbours, no pets, no toys, nothing much but what you carried around with yourself.

But it must have left its mark. In some cases consciously. I liked primroses and violets in hedge banks. I liked the lane through which I walked to and from school. I liked the school, with its rows of wild flowers in fish-paste pots on the window-sills. I became completely hooked on Kenneth Grahame's *The Wind in the Willows*, which the teacher read aloud to us. I had enjoyed measuring myself against an enormous thistle which grew, and grew, in the field in front of the cottage.

More important probably was the subconscious effect. I had not been born to solitary survival; I had not had training in self-sufficiency; I was not much of a handyman; I had little or no mechanical instinct. But I had the *experience* of Devon, albeit that it had been twenty-five years before, albeit that some of it had not been very happy. It had all gone in. It must have counted for something.

5

Watching

'Name an active volcano.'
'Mount Vesuvius.'

Isn't that the answer which nine people out of ten would give? (Those who don't live near another active volcano, that is.) Most of us do not live near Mount Vesuvius, so why is it such a part of our common general knowledge? Perhaps because it is one of the best documented geographical events in ancient history. We all (well, again, most of us) know about the horror in AD 79, when two whole Roman cities, Herculaneum and Pompeii, were engulfed in a matter of hours. This knowledge is cemented into our common memory largely, possibly, because Pompeii must be one of the most-visited places on the tourist itinerary. We don't know much about what Vesuvius did before and after AD 79, but *we do know that eruptions happen.* We see the evidence on our Italian coach holiday.

Hence we marvel at the obvious fact that thousands of people were prepared to live around this massive mound of menace, this womb of cataclysm. They must have known; the eruption of 79 was not the first. There have been others since. And people are *still* prepared to live there.

Now come forward nearly nineteen hundred years to 1952. To the small seaside town of Lynmouth, at the confluence of the East and West Lyn Rivers. Everybody knows that if you have rivers and confluences and gorges and rain (North Devon is never short of rain), floods are *likely*, to say the least. Nevertheless, people were prepared to live there.

This was Devon. Everybody knew that nothing much happened in Devon. Nothing in particular had happened since the Norman Conquest, and not much before that. Hence the joke about the introduction of decimal coinage in 1971. As one know-all remarked to a brow-furrowed companion, 'Daun' ee worry abote that thur decimal coinege, mah dere. 'Twon't get done yer for yurrs yet.'

So it didn't bother anybody much that the countryside around Lynmouth was honeycombed with deep narrow lanes; bridges were old and low; many cottages perched close to river banks; the two main rivers joined on the edge of the very town itself, and flowed into the Bristol Channel down a narrow gorge. It didn't bother anybody much when it rained a lot in August. Around Exmoor it usually did. But the moss and the heather normally accounted for that – like gigantic blotting paper.

When everyone went to bed on the night of 15th-16th August, 1952, they had no idea that nine inches or rain had been falling, or were going to fall, in 24 hours. The blotting paper didn't work any more. Higher streams could not cope with the volume of water. The lower the tide of trouble descended, the bigger and stronger it became, as more tributaries of the East and West Lyn added their own swollen contribution. Steep-sided channels only made the water more terrible and unstoppable. Nothing was proof against it – trees, bridges, boulders, houses were hurled like corks down towards Lynmouth, where the East Lyn and the West Lyn joined to envelop the whole town.

Bad enough in daylight; at night it must have been horrific. Countless animals were lost. Twenty-eight bridges went. Whole rows of cottages. The famous Rhenish tower in Lynmouth Harbour vanished in seconds. Thirty-four people died. That may not sound very much among the awful statistics of tsunamis today, but Lynmouth was not a large town. It was an old and intimate one. Most people knew most other people; nearly every family lost somebody.

The Lynmouth Flood came to acquire an almost Biblical signif-icance for the local population. I have seen no documentary evidence for this, but the story went around in 1972 that a BBC camera team came to Lynmouth to make a film to commemorate the twentieth anniversary of the Flood. They had to pack up and go home; nobody would talk to them.

The stream that flowed past New Mill was not dignified with the name 'river'; it appeared on the Ordnance Survey map as 'Ilkerton Water'. But it joined the two Lyns lower down, and it was just as capable of bringing menace and destruction; it was only a matter of comparative scale. As I said earlier, the house was saved, so we were told, by a haystack that stood between the oncoming deluge and the western wall. The stack was shunted against the wall, but took the brunt of the water's attack.

The two inmates survived too. The house, remember, was built into the side of a hill, where the mill leet flowed. A small landing window opened at the back on to this slope, so the elderly couple who lived there were able to scramble out on to relatively dry land, and crawl up the slope in the dark to safety. Sounds simple enough now, but, if you stop to think of frightened old ladies and distraught old men, feeble muscles, night clothes, probably bare feet, and the dark, not to mention the noise (many eye-witnesses testified to the roar of the water), you begin to realise what a terrible experience it must have been.

I was not frightened by this story, but I was naturally considerably impressed by it. You have to see flood water before you begin to get some idea of what it is like. When I did see it, I was surprised to note that it was not particularly loud, and not turbulent either. Nevertheless, it had signs of its own. The water went brown, and it went flat. The silence was sinister. The roar as the water tore through a narrow, rock-filled gorge at Lynmouth must have been a hundred times worse.

Of course, I did not see floodwater on anything like the scale of the awful night of the 15th August. In my time, the water rose, more than once, but it never came in over the doorstep. Even so, it concentrated the mind wonderfully well to stand just inside the doorstep and watch it licking at the *outside* of the doorstep, just a couple of inches from the top.

So, either as a bachelor or, later, as a family man, I never had to get out the mops and buckets, and for that I was always grateful. But it all taught you to have a great respect for the river; you could never afford to become *blasé* about it. It would have been tempting Fate.

By the same token we had to teach the boys to have respect too. The two stepsons, Christopher and Martin, were aged eight and six when they first arrived, so they caught on pretty quickly. But Stephen was born there, and we obviously had to be very careful with him.

I fancy that, today, a health and safety expert would take one look at the set-up and have a fit. No barriers, no safety ropes, no fences. Slippery stones, large rocks, congested hedges on the far bank with sudden drops straight into the water – if it had been today, we would have stood a good chance of being prosecuted.

But the boys learned, and we trusted them. We could rely on Christopher and Martin to keep an eye on Stephen when we weren't around. Honestly, I can not recall a single serious worry relating to any of them. Not even when Martin fell in – three times in one afternoon. It was barely nine inches deep. He simply hauled himself out, muttered whatever curses ten-year-old boys mutter to them-selves, and went indoors to change.

When the river ran high, that was a different matter, naturally. But again, they had the sense to stay away. And they were probably healthily frightened too. Who wouldn't be? It was a frightening sight. They would have been very unlikely to be out anyway, wouldn't they, because, as likely as not, it would have been pouring with rain.

Most of the time, then, everything was pretty all right. There were umpteen things for boys to do in and around a nine-inch stream, and they did them. The Water Rat, beside his river, used to love messing about in boats. The boys did their share of messing with model boats, stones, dams, banks, and I don't know what. Christopher took up fishing, and landed his fair contribution of trout for the supper table.

Visitors who came down in spring and summer used to take in the house, the cobbles, the tinkling water, throw up their hands in wonderment, and say, 'Idyllic! Idyllic!'

Well, yes, on a warm sunny day it could indeed be very nice.

Animal life abounded. Tame animals obviously – cattle in the field on the other side. Sheep up on the hills. We had a young Labrador for a while, whose speciality was eating my books on the lower shelves – what you might call a voracious reader. We had a cat too – name of Gilbert (I don't remember why; it was a female).

Out at the back we used to see minks now and then. Voles too (wasn't Ratty actually a vole?) Wasps and bees galore. Even more galore were the horseflies, which rose in wrath when you attempted to cut the grass in summer. Christopher got stung by one, and it turned so nasty that we had to take him to the cottage hospital in Lynton, where he passed out before they had touched him with the needle.

I learned to recognise some birds, like magpies and jays. Up till then the only birds I knew the difference between were robins and golden eagles. I did once surprise a heron wading in the stream very early one morning. The opening of the bedroom window disturbed him. He hoisted himself into the air without the slightest sign of haste, and flew off. If you can flap wings in a lofty, disdainful manner, he managed it. (Again, my knowledge of *The Wind in the Willows* reminded me of a reference to herons in the first chapter, when Ratty was telling Mole river stories – 'about herons, and how particular they were whom they spoke to'. So Kenneth Grahame had clearly formed the same impression of herons as I had.)

I think the most prestigious wild creature we saw was the occasional otter. In those days the papers were full of the threat to the otter population. I understand that that does not apply now.

Horses were frequent, almost regular. Not pulling carts or ploughs, of course; Devon was not *that* far behind the times. For all that Devon farmers have a reputation for being conservative, sunk in habit and tradition, suspicious of change, and generally pretty ornery, it has often struck me that they have a knack of latching on to whatever technological change that comes their way. Quickly. They are good at them too; they have transferred their instinct and general mechanical knackery from scythes and ploughshares and fan belts on traction engines to diesel engines and combine harvesters.

(By the same token, no organisation could be more conservative or reactionary than the Catholic Church, but they have been jumping on the technology bandwagon ever since they saw the importance of the compass and the printing press. I bet you didn't know that they have a patron saint for television.)

Nevertheless, despite this skill with machines, Devon farmers have sustained their interest in and fondness for horses. Exmoor is perfect riding country. And not only for farmers. Horsy young women straight from posh convent school sixth forms, pre-teens in dome-like black helmets festooned with rosettes from gymkhanas, the hacking-jacket-and-cheese-cutter-cap brigade, the double-barrelled hunt ball clan. Towns, villages, and big manor houses have their shows and their meets in total independence, almost disdain, of the rest of the world. If you want to join in, that's fine; if you don't, that's too bad, and shut the gate when you go. It is darkly suggested that the anti-blood sport legislation has made very few dents in the fondness of Devonians for the pleasures of the chase.

Now, how did all this affect us? We didn't own horses. I have never been on a horse in my life, and have never had the slightest yearning to be on one. We couldn't afford riding lessons for the boys – and they wouldn't have wanted them anyway. All three have shown a marked indifference over the years to the vast majority of those activities which are popularly supposed to provide adventure, foster team spirit, stretch you to the limit, and generally enhance your character. (Though Christopher, to his eternal credit, did complete the 55-mile Ten Tors Expedition in his last year at school. Martin gave up after coming home soaked by snow up to his waist on the first practice walk. Stephen managed the 45-mile job, but his hips creaked for years afterwards.) Abseiling, rock-climbing, caving, orienteering, and snow-holing have left them stone cold – to coin a phrase.

So, to repeat, how did all this business about horses affect us? Because, every so often, the hunt would come past. Now, the days are long gone when rich landowners could gallop with their fellow-members all over their tenants' fields without a by-your-leave. One of the many useless pieces of information I gleaned from the study of eighteenth-century history was the fact that one aristocrat, even richer than the rest, could ride through three counties without ever having to leave his own property.

To be honest, I don't suppose the horses did much damage to our garden. There wasn't much of it for a start, and it was so littered with bramble and stones that the track was a much better pathway – and it was, technically, a right of way.

What I did find annoying was not the activities so much as the attitudes, and here I betray myself as one of the plebs, jealous of the nobs with their superior ways. These riders may have behaved themselves in a legal sense, but they also behaved themselves as if they owned the place, and we were part of the furniture.

If you look at the famous paintings of the wagon trains crossing the Great Plains of America in the nineteenth century, you see Indians, yes, but they only gather in little groups of silent witnesses on the edges of the picture. Not really part of the drama of the Great West Epic. Incidental. Well, I used to feel a bit like that.

And that was only the riders. It was the followers who were the real pain. We soon discovered that following the hunt was an established, and very popular, Devon pastime. Pursued with the eagerness, devotion, and single-mindness of a professional football crowd.

Of course they could not stumble breathlessly at the heels, or rather the hooves, of the horses, but they flexed every muscle to get as close as they could. In cars and Land-Rovers they roared around quiet lanes, leapt out at minute lay-bys, leaned on bramble-bound gates, focused binoculars on a distant hillside, picked up the track, rushed back to their driving-seats, and roared off again.

If they were on foot, a tiny lane which everyone knew was a right of way was an obvious and irresistible avenue. It was a wonder some of them didn't break their neck at the tight bends or over the jutting, slippery rocks.

And even *that* would have been tolerable. But when they reached the bottom and fished out their binoculars again, they would go anywhere on the property in order to get a better view of the hills above and around. (Rather like mobile phone owners desperate to find the best place for a call.) Totally absorbed. The path, which was indeed a right of way, was not seen as a designated route but as a means of entry. They clambered everywhere. The house might not have been there.

I was a bit short with one or two of them. I think they were more surprised than cross. Certainly not contrite.

A final word on the last member of the animal kingdom we became acquainted with – the tourist. Again, most of them did no wrong; it is the oddities and stupidities one remembers. Many of course were courteous and interested, and we had some pleasant conversations. But one gazed in a mixture of wonderment and amusement at the little crocodiles of bright young things who had, presumably, parked their cars somewhere at the top, and were sampling the countryside. T-shirts, flimsy mini-skirts, nylon stockings, bare arms, stiletto heels. I doubt if there were a couple of handbags between half a dozen of them, much less a tiny rucksack. No precautions, no provision for incidents, no idea of what Exmoor weather could do.

Then there was there were the cliché-coiners. If they stopped to speak, their conversation was full of words and phrases like 'quaint', 'gorgeous', 'away from the rat race', 'I've always wanted to live in a place like this'.

Again, it seems never to have crossed the mind of some of them that people actually did. At warm weekends, or during holidays, we were in the habit of leaving both windows and doors open. Not only did they stand back and gaze at the house as if it were part of a rural display at a county show, gasping with amazement or pointing out marvellous features to each other. It was not unknown for one or two to come up to the front door, and without knocking, put their heads inside and gaze around – again, as if it were an exhibit

– and again breathing teeth-grinding platitudes.

We often wondered what would have been their reaction if we had wandered up their manicured front garden, and, without asking, put our heads inside their front door, and said 'how quaint' as we surveyed their fitted carpet and potted plants.

6

Clearing

There is a very old story about the American tourist who was visiting one of the Oxford or Cambridge colleges. Naturally he thought the architecture was 'marrvellus'. Anything older than the Declaration of Independence is always a winner when you want to make a Yank's jaw drop. But this man was even more impressed with the gardens, and particularly the lawns. As you know, they grace nearly every court in every college – squares, rectangles, triangles, and the famous circular one at Christ's College in Cambridge. Our visitor was both astounded and mystified by the symmetry and billiard-table smoothness of the grass. They made bowling greens look like ploughed fields.

He happened to see one of the college gardeners at work on some flower beds, and approached him.

'Say, how do you get these lawns so goddammed purrfect? What is the secret?'

The gardener, who had been asked this question a thousand times, stood up and looked his visitor up and down, assessing him with quizzical accuracy.

'Well, it's very easy, sir. All you have to do is get a piece of grass; then you cut and roll it for four hundred years.'

Well, get as far away from those college lawns as it is conceivably possible to get, and you might, you might just, begin to imagine what the ground around New Mill looked like.

Ironically, the one thing they might have had in common was age. The colleges can boast histories of three, four, five hundred years – in some cases even more. New Mill had three hundred

53

years behind it. Ken found a reference to it in a dusty tome in Lynton Public Library, which mentioned a tax return for 1674. As I explained before, if it said 'New Mill' (and it did), it is logical to suppose that, at some distant time before that, there must have been an 'Old Mill'. Even more provocative, the entry in Domesday Book for the Manor of Lyn also mentions a *'novum molendinum'* – a 'new mill'. So the original old mill must have been even older than that. And Domesday is over nine hundred years old. If our American friend had known that, he would have been truly dumbfounded at the thought. Gee whiz!

Incidentally, the words 'dusty tome' in the previous paragraph conjure up a picture of a pretty dusty author too, don't they? When you find out that the author was the Revd. John Chanter, you nod your head knowingly and say, 'Yet another of these fusty nineteenth-century clergymen who had a lot of spare time on their hands as ministers of a moribund Anglican Church.' True, there were then many energetic religious movements – Quakers, Evangelicals, Methodists, and later the apologists for a revived Anglo-Catholicism (the Oxford Movement). But the official, central, controlling, permanent hub of the nation's religious life was the Church of England, of course, the Anglican Church, the Established Church. Well, it may have been all those things, but it was not much else. It had long since run out of steam (ironic in the new steam age).

Anyway, Chanter seems a typical example of a minister of that institution, and he would have remained so in my mind if I had not come across another reference to him, or rather *from* him, in a completely different connection. He left an account of his childhood. Part of that childhood had been spent as a junior pupil at West Buckland School, on the edge of Exmoor – although in those early days it was known as the Devon County School (long story). Well, in 1864, there was an outbreak of scarlet fever in the school (an all-too-familiar scourge in those days). Not only did they have to close the school; they had to fumigate it too. That meant farming the boys out in neighbouring accommodation all around the area. It happened that Chanter found himself, a junior, boarded out with a lot of boys older than himself.

It was a long hot summer, and there was nothing to do – well, no class lessons anyway. A later headmaster of the County School once drily observed that 'healthy, vigorous boys do not do nothing'. So these boys got up to all sorts of mischief, and young Chanter tagged along – and probably enhanced his education no end. Expeditions out on to the moor; hunting, poaching, getting dirty, sliding down precipitous scree slopes, and eating and drinking all sorts of things they were not supposed to.

I find it refreshing to read that a member of the mid-century rural dog-collar brigade (a pillar of respectability, you would have thought) had spent part at any rate of his childhood doing what he shouldn't have been doing. It almost began to restore your respect for stuffy ancient Anglican vicars.

Anyway, let us look at the 'estate' (or rather the state) of New Mill when I arrived. I read somewhere once that, if a field is left to itself for twenty years, by the end of that time, the natural vegetation will have re-established itself. Well, when Ken bought it, it had been derelict for just over ten years, so it was not covered with deciduous forest. But it was at the mercy of bramble and weed. Boundary walls had tumbled. Cobbles in front of the house were covered to a depth of getting on for a foot. The outside toilet was a shell. The shippens were a mass of trapeziums; all the right angles had slipped. That was when *I* first saw it. When Ken first came across it, the situation must have been far worse. It says a lot for his imagination and enterprise that he entertained the mere thought of taking it on.

Nowadays you see council workmen busy clearing hedges, ditches, roadside verges, and any other space that the council deem to be worth clearing. We have become used to the hard hats, ear-pads, eye-guards, leather gloves, mechanical rucksacks, cutters, sprayers, strimmers, miles of cable, gadgets like instruments of medieval torture, and huge contraptions like Martian war machines. DIY shops now are chock full of legions of various devices which are supposed to take the labour out of what I am describing – cordless, plugless, battery-less, petrol-less, weightless, and of course accident-proof.

All Ken and I had was shears, rakes, and sickles (they call them 'grass-hooks' round here). And when you have cleared it all, there was the small matter of disposal. To give you some idea, the oldest brambles could be as thick as a man's thumb; creepers like convolvulus could tie brambles and weeds together in insoluble knots thicker than any Gordian puzzle. So cutting them was only the beginning of the problem. Waist-high nettles waited to sting bare arms as you stretched to reach one clump or haul out another. Horse flies, disturbed and angry, added to the entertainment.

It could take the pair of us two or three days to clear New Mill Lane. I must have been a sucker for punishment, because one year I took it into my head to clear the whole of the mill leet behind the house. It must have been thirty or forty yards long. The house had not been occupied since 1952, and I believe that the mill had fallen into disuse long before that. So the bramble, fern, and creeper over and around the leet made New Mill Lane look like Kew Gardens. Looking back, I can't think what possessed me even to contemplate it. The hours I spent on it, and I had little to show for it. I did manage to expose the ledge along which the leet had run, but the dream of forging a decorous grassy bank – with perhaps a primrose or two – remained a sweat-soaked dream. I never finished it.

Bramble, fern, and creeper, however, were only the beginning.

Before long, we made the acquaintance of Russian rhubarb. It grew prolifically on the far bank of the stream. Curiously not on the side where the house was. I use the name 'Russian rhubarb' because that was what Ken called it. I have never since had cause to question it.

Till now. As I am embarked on a book about this house, I thought it appropriate to do just a little research, to give perhaps a tiny measure of greater authority to what I am writing. So heigh-ho for the net. As always you find yourself in a maze, or a maelstrom, or a glut, or an Aladdin's cave (whatever feeble cliché mixed metaphor you fancy) of information.

I was looking for something which would tell me about how and why this plant was a pest and a threat. Because I understand that it is. I seemed to be doomed to frustration. Besides Russian rhubarb, I found German rhubarb, Chinese rhubarb, Indian rhubarb, even Arizona rhubarb. I was invited to 'buy rhubarb pictures'. (Sent no doubt in plain covers.) And there were plenty more lurking in later website titles. But they didn't tell me much, because the majority of them were about recipes – Turkish rhubarb root, rhubarb vodka liqueur (God Almighty!), and Henriette's Herbal Homepage (a charmingly genteel antidote).

I had almost given up when I tried typing in 'Wild rhubarb', and came across 'Giant Rhubarb'. It was introduced before the War into Western Ireland, much to the later regret of farmers and gardeners. Its large leaves blocked the sun from neighbouring plants; its prolific seeds were spread by birds; and it soon became 'a potentially invasive, colony-forming threat to native flora'. And it proved 'extremely difficult to eradicate'. (You can say that again.)

I suppose it spread to the West Country because of the migrating birds. Ireland is not that far away across the Irish Sea.

I pored over the photographs on the website. It looked like our plant all right.

Not much help though. Even if I had known all that when I began at New Mill, it would not have made my work any easier. The best I could do was to hack away with the grass-hook, kick the debris into the water, and make sure I did not slip into it afterwards. The bank was very narrow and steep. The boundary wire of the neighbouring farmer's field was only about five feet from the stream.

It was a never-ending task. You had about a couple of days to stand on the other side and admire your handiwork, before the stuff began to recover. You could almost see it growing.

At least though it was not a tough plant, like, say, couch grass or ivy or bramble. It did succumb to the blade with relatively little struggle. You could see progress after an hour's work.

With knotweed you did not have that satisfaction.

It just shows you what an aid to coincidence the internet is. I was doing that research on Russian rhubarb when I came across knotweed. Apparently the two plants have many features in common (don't ask me to name them; it's as much as I can do to get these few facts down on paper). The website offered the stark warning that, if you plan to get rid of it, you must *on no account* pull it out or dig it up. What on earth do you do then? You cut it, that's what. And it's thick and it's tough.

Searching for consolation, I turned to a 'proper' website for 'Japanese knotweed'. Because that is where it comes from. A mighty long way. No wonder it is tough and resilient.

I found no comfort. Japanese knotweed is not only practically impervious to the sweatiest efforts of humble householders with grass-hooks in North Devon; it is capable of fracturing 'concrete foundations, flood defences, roads, paving, retaining walls, and architectural sites'. Makes you wonder how they get anything built at all. In 2012 (or rather in the previous year or two), they discovered it on a patch of ground earmarked for the London Olympics. To eradicate it cost the authorities £130 million. Well, that's what it said.

There is now, we are told, a hope. The boffins have traced a bug which eats nothing but knotweed. It originates, conveniently, in Japan. So there is some justice. It is called the wild Japanese psyllid insect – *aphalara itadori*. It is planned to organise 'controlled release' of it this year, 2016. I don't know how you can 'control' the activities of a fertile creature like an insect, but we shall see.

So here were two plants which were notorious for their pernicious potential, and New Mill had both of them. And of course none of what I have explained above was any help to us in the late 1960's. It was all a mite troublesome.

However, it did help to put things in perspective. Other weeds and unwanted growths were child's play in comparison, and of course we did much appreciate the 'legitimate' flora – the daffodils, bluebells, snowdrops, foxglove, campion, wild garlic, rose bay willow herb, and all the rest. The primroses were a delight. As we were in a place which was not short of water, we were not short of primroses. (Some years later, when I moved house to a village near Barnstaple, I took some plants to put in the garden, imagining and looking forward to similar nodding clumps of delicate yellow all over the place. No such luck. My plants steadily shrank and became wizened parodies of the glorious shows at New Mill. They grew, and grow, in their thousands in the banks along main roads and along country lanes, but they wouldn't grow in my garden.)

I just said that New Mill wasn't short of water. It wasn't short of stones either. Built up on the ground, strewn about the ground, impeding our progress around the ground, and hiding just under the ground. It made gardening doubly hard. In fact, in the end, we didn't grow much. Even when we got rid of some of the stones, they were often replaced by persistent molehills.

I tried to cut the grass at the end of the house, where the haystack had been, and I bought a second-hand mower to attempt it. The hidden stones played havoc with the cutter blades and sent seismic shocks up the arms. But some progress was made. We did manage to clear enough ground to enable us to have a decorous tea party now and then. There was also a gap in a bank right in front of the house, which provided another modest stretch of grass sloping down to the water's edge. You couldn't balance a cup of tea on it, and getting tiny tables and deckchairs into some kind of level plane took a deal of patience and joggling. Nor could you honestly call it a lawn. Still, it was green, clean, and comforting. And it was all ours.

The stones, though, did offer some kind of therapy. I discovered that, if you are among thousands of assorted-shaped stones, and if you have some space, and if you have just a little spare time, you will find an excuse to build a wall. It doesn't have to be a big one – four or five courses will do. But wherever you put it, it looks tidy, neat, organised, purposeful. It looks as if you are in charge. As I said, most therapeutic.

One particular excuse like this sent me to the back of the house, where the ground (half strangled by the knotweed) stretches up to the mill leet. For some reason which now escapes me, I had developed an interested in roses. I had always liked them, of course; as a historian and as a sucker for anything sentimental like this, I was of the opinion that the rose was the queen of English flowers.

In the newsagents I started looking at magazine pages about roses. I might even have bought a little paperback handbook. I devoured the photographs. I let my imagination run riot when we visited garden centres (or nurseries, as we called them then). One particular vision caught my eye – blue roses. I wanted a blue rose.

Now, I hope I have by now demonstrated to you that the last place you would have wanted to start a tame, well-manicured, rich-soiled garden was New Mill. But when you have a craze, that doesn't stop you. I was going to grow some blue roses.

I attacked part of the bank below the mill leet. Clearly, I couldn't expect these plants to survive among the brambles and the ferns, and putting them among the knotweed would have been a sentence of death. So I was going to excavate a special shelter for them. Hacked out of the bank, lined with yet more stones, and filled with well-sifted soil and fertiliser. Ken took one look and christened them 'the gun emplacements'.

Nevertheless, I planted two blue roses. And they grew. And they bloomed. Not for very long, I must admit, but long enough to give me a deal of satisfaction. I had taken on the knotweed, the bank, the stones, the fern and bramble, and I had produced something. I forget how many seasons they survived after that. Probably only two or three at most. But that does not matter. I grew my blue roses. And I can see them in my mind's eye now. Two blue roses alone in the Exmoor wilderness. It's quite an image, isn't it?

It is quite likely that anybody reading this – anybody with a smattering of proper knowledge about gardens and stones and water and near-derelict cottages – would say to himself a dozen times, 'Why on earth did he do that?: Why on earth didn't he do so-and-so? Surely he should have tumbled to such-and-such? All he had to do was buy this or hire that.'

Well, yes, he probably would. But I was there, and I didn't know. I was simply pleased to be there, and I was pleased to return there at the start of every holiday. I found it totally absorbing, and it never occurred to me to chuck it in. As G.K. Chesterton said, 'If a thing is worth doing, it is worth doing badly.'

Exmoor bridge

7

Living

I work as a school archivist. Well, I do now. I was a teacher for the greater part of my working life. When the teaching dried up, I was asked if I would like to start and run a school archive. It is, admittedly, only part-time work. And I am not professionally qualified for it. But I have been doing the job for over twenty years, so I can fairly claim to have learned something about it. There are always surprises, of course; that is one of the reasons why it is interesting. But there are also a lot of things which, through repetition, become familiar.

One of them is the misconception that many people have of what the job involves. We all build up our collection of pat clichés about other people's work. It might be because of one single stark experience of it – say, a traumatic half-hour in a dentist's chair, which can colour one's opinion of the entire profession for a long time. More likely, it is the cumulative result of a thousand scanty glances at it, usually as a result of television, film drama, biased reporting in the newspaper, over-the-fence chat with a neighbour, or the laying down of the law by the local saloon-bar know-all.

So we all know that teachers spend their time saying, 'Get out your text-books and turn to the next chapter.' Politicians make pompous speeches and tell lies. Bankers get enormous bonuses; if they make a pig's breakfast of their job, they get even bigger bonuses to make them leave. Soldier recruits use up half their day spitting on the toecaps of their boots, and the other half being sworn at by a sergeant-major. Headmasters in 'posh' schools wear gowns and mortar-boards all the time. And so on and so on.

Archivists deal with old documents. We all know that old documents can be musty and dusty, and that they are kept in equally musty and dusty cupboards and lofts that nobody ever looks into. So the man (or woman, in theory, but the cliché is always about a man, and he has to be an old one) who works there has the must and dust blowing off on to his tired suit, till he begins to look like an archive himself. Archivists don't work in rooms or offices; they work in 'cubby holes', usually in basements or garrets.

But now and again, a colleague will have given a passing thought to the topic, and will be fair-minded enough to work out that there must be more to it than that. He doesn't quite know what that is, and he has his suspicions about the value of an archive, but at least he would like to find out.

So he fixes you with a gimlet glance, screws up his eyes, and says, 'What do you actually *do*?'

Well, here is not the place to answer that question. I have published five books in an attempt to offer some kind of answer to it, and you can buy them on the net. No, what I am on about now is the fact that a similar question could be framed concerning the place I have been writing about.

You know – New Mill was like this or like that; you had this problem or you had that one; you had to do so-and-so in order to survive. Yes. But when you got around to ordinary living, what did you actually *do*? Why were you there?

Good question. It's always the simple ones that are the most awkward. Like the child who asked, 'Why do teachers put a tick when it's right and a cross when it's wrong?' It generated a lot of column space in at least one learned educational journal. I don't think it was ever resolved to the satisfaction of everybody, but the pedants had a good time.

So – what the devil *was* I doing there?

Enjoying a change is the first thing that comes to mind. New Mill was light years away from a top flat in a block in Kingston upon Thames. It had space. It had privacy. I could go to my front door and just stand and look. You don't stand at the door of your flat and look; there is nothing to see.

It was far more open to the elements. You could see and feel the weather. It was, quite literally, on your doorstep. It was somehow more normal and natural. Not always comfortable, but when it was good it was very good. Of course, when it was bad it was bloody awful. But you did run a much bigger gamut of situations and emotions. There were more things to feel. You were covering the whole scale; you weren't missing anything.

You were less dependent on so many things. You had to be; they weren't there. The television for a start. (True, we got it several years later, but, because of the position of the house deep in a valley, the reception was never 20:20, as you might say.) The telephone. If you wanted to make a call, you had to walk well over a mile to the nearest phone box. Carpets. Yes, I had some, but not many, and not in what could be called mint condition. It was dusters and brooms, not hoovers. The same could be said of the furniture – the random harvest of Ken's trips to the auction rooms.

It should go without saying, but, just in case anybody under forty assumes that computers and laptops have always been with us, there *were no* computers, laptops, games, touch-screens, i-pads, a-pads, blogs, tweets, floppigrams, brextexts, selfies, effies, boffies, toffees, or anything else. They had not been invented – well, not for the general public. Mind you, they were for that reason not available in Kingston flats either.

So much more was up to you (or, nowadays, 'down' to you; now where did that change come from?). Cooking obviously. If you were feeling a bit below par, there was no Indian restaurant one way, and no fish and chip shop the other. If you didn't cook it, it was bread and cheese for supper. The same with heating. I couldn't afford electric heating. And if I could, the feeble plaster and dodgy stonework would not have sustained wall heaters. Even if it could, I couldn't afford to get an electric engineer all the way down New Mill Lane to do the work. If you wanted to get warm, you filled the paraffin heaters and you lugged in some logs from outside (assuming that you had prudently sawn some up as a reserve, and assuming too that you had a spare five-gallon drum and a spare gas cylinder that you had lugged down the hill the day before). You didn't have a gas poker; it was down in a pre-natal position and paper and kindling and blowing at the right time.

I suppose, looking back, it was a bit like Robinson Crusoe. You did it all yourself and you compromised and you made do and patched things up and tied them together. But there was so much satisfaction waiting for you if you actually succeeded in making everything work. You took more pleasure in modest achievements. You came to realise that many things were not indispensable.

You were so absorbed in solving problems and meeting difficulties that you had no time to spare for contemplating all the other problems and difficulties.

Being independent meant that you were a committee of one; you could organise your day exactly as you wished. The only proviso to this came when Ken was also in residence. In fulfilment of our original agreement, I had to make myself available to help when he needed it. Holding a wash-basin in place while he did the plugging and screwing; being on the other end of a two-man saw; easing the weight of stones, branches, beams; holding the light as he groped in dark corners (still humming the Pilgrims' Chorus); just being around to hold the rags and pass the tools when he was engaged in a particularly tricky or nasty job. As he once observed, 'Work like this is so much more bearable when there are two of you at it.'

But, to be fair, Ken did not monopolise me. I had simply to keep an eye open for the times when he clearly needed me. The rest of the days were my own. And of course, when Ken was not there, every single day was my own – all of it.

I was always up early; there was no need, or temptation, to stay in bed. There was the day, waiting for me. I had come two hundred miles to enjoy it, so it was stupid to lie in. If the weather allowed, there was, as I said, the shower under the sycamore. Ever taken a shower surrounded by a hundred clumps of primroses? Or had a shave at a bedroom (later a bathroom) window from which you see a stream, hawthorn hedges, cows, sheep, a hill with a track going up on the side of it? A jay, a magpie, a heron? If you were lucky, even some sun, though not direct; it did not shine direct on to the house till midday. At such times, even the Russian rhubarb on the other bank did not look unwelcome.

Breakfast was a doddle – boiled eggs, toast (I had a gas stove at least – thanks to the much-lugged cylinders), plenty of marmalade, and tea ad lib. Again, if the weather allowed, it was a cushion on the doorstep, and contemplate the stream.

What did the morning have to offer? Well, naturally, washing up and bedmaking, bringing in logs for the evening fire, topping up the paraffin heater. Shaking a coir mat or two. Sweeping, of course. Always sweeping. Maybe up to the top of the hill to see if Stan Marsh had delivered the groceries, or to take up an empty gas cylinder. Say hallo to John Leworthy, the farmer whose house was up at the top too, beside the old railway bridge.

What was on the cards for the morning? Some painting or varnishing. Rigging up a more accessible clothes line. Clearing another square yard of the covered-over cobbles. Washing out some smalls.

Lunch. Always on time. Don't let your routine go awry.

Afternoon – a fair-sized carpentry project with battening and hardboard (which Ken had had delivered the previous week). When I say 'carpentry' I mean something pretty primitive with hammer, saws, screw-drivers, and hand-drills. I don't know a dovetail from a half-hitch. Everything I made was massive; it wasn't gracious, but my word, it would hold together.

Break for tea after four o'clock. Never go on for too long. After tea maybe tackle some simple construction with stones – say, at the water's edge, especially where the mill leet ran out under the track and into the stream. But never, never get too involved. Work like this can be therapeutic, but it can also be addictive. It's hard to stop. Like looking up something on the internet today.

From then on you have to keep your eye sharply on the clock. You have to clear up whatever job you have been doing. Don't be upset if you haven't made the progress you were hoping for (you never do), and try and arrange that, when you come back to it the next day, you will be able to see exactly where to start in again.

You have to prepare the ingredients for dinner. It must be a solid meal. You have worked up an appetite; you must feed it, or you will not be up to much in the morning. (On your own, remember? Think ahead. Think of what you need to keep going.)

It is the end of the day. You are dirty. So is it upstairs to the wash-basin you helped Ken to instal, or out to the shower under the sycamore? But before that you have to light the fire. (You have of course collected enough kindling to keep you going for a few days.) The grate is old, the grid is old, the whole damn thing is old. So it is cantankerous; it will need all your powers of cunning and persuasion to get it going.

Then, at last, you feel you can trust it to be left while you have that shower.

Finally, cooking. But keep the routine running. Keep the framework of the day in mind. One of the main reasons you have come here is to enjoy a good meal, a good drink, and a good hour in front of a good fire with a good book.

So never let the work get bigger than you. The trouble with a house like New Mill is that, before you are barely into a job, you discover that, before you can finish, you really need to do something more basic in order to make the job easier. But, when you get stuck into the more basic job, you find that there is a problem which is holding you up in the remedying of that basic job. You are in danger of falling into the grip of Obsessive Domestic Repair Perfectionitis. You are in danger of coming to the conclusion that the only real solution to your original problem is to rebuild the house. Time to stop, no matter at what stage the work is. Stop.

So, if you are lucky, and if you have exercised superhuman self-control, and if you have not left yourself with only nine and a half minutes to grill that pork chop, mash the potatoes, fry the tomatoes and mushrooms, and maybe shove a rice pudding in the oven, and if you have not let the fire go out, you can at last sit down and tuck in.

That should leave you with just enough time to wash up, make some coffee, sit in front of what, with luck, should be now be a respectable blaze, and read your book.

Bed at half-past nine. A lot to do tomorrow. And the paraffin heater to see to before you go upstairs. A minute or two to stand at the door and listen to the stream. And you should sleep pretty well.

The fact that I describe a typical day at New Mill does not mean that every single day was the same. Time never staled its infinite variety, to coin a phrase.

There was the whole of North Devon outside. Bus trips to Barnstaple were that much more attractive because of their comparative rarity. Plenty of shops, real shops. You could go to an old-fashioned stationer. At the top of the High Street was a grocer's which still had mahogany counters. Ken once took me to an ancient foundry to check up on some metal work he had commissioned. (You see? I would never have known anything about that. Ken had sized up the job; he knew what was wanted; he knew what he could manage and what he couldn't; he knew where to go to get the service he needed; he knew enough to explain, argue, and even haggle if necessary. He was no spendthrift.)

Lunch we would often take in Bromley's – a delightful hang-over from all those genteel Tudor restaurants and posh corner houses from the 'forties and 'fifties, where you could still get meat and two veg. It's a Chinese restaurant now – quite a good one actually.

Incidentally, if this should give you the impression that Barnstaple was a deal behind the times, you would be right. But if you wanted something in a real time-slip, you should have tried Bideford – it was almost pre-war. That is meant to sound not critical but affectionate. You have to be eighty now to remember the War, but it is worth remembering that, in 1967, when I first arrived in Devon, the War had finished only twenty-two years before. Ex-servicemen were in their forties, not their nineties. As I sit here and write this, it is a shock to realise that I began at New Mill nearly fifty years ago.

However, Barnstaple. . . If we went in on a Friday, a compelling port of call was the cattle market. And I don't mean an empty space with rusting iron fence-poles and gates all over the place, but a proper cattle market, with cattle. Full of well-covered men in waist-coats and tweed jackets and clamped-on caps, with watch-chains and side-whiskers, itching to get the business of the day over so that they could adjourn to a nearby hostelry – and there was no shortage of those.

People still dealt with ha'pennies and half-crowns and bobs and tanners. Notes were for a pound or ten shillings. You rarely saw a fiver, much less a tenner.

Farmers were sophisticated enough to deal in cheques for their business, and they took cheques very seriously. A local optician once told me that middle-aged farmers did not like to be seen wearing glasses in case it showed signs of physical weakness. But, when it came to writing a cheque, they all put their specs on.

In case I have suggested that Devon farmers in those days might have been not quite up to speed compared with their urban counterparts with their smart shoes and their jutting cuffs, let me correct it at once by saying that anyone who entered into any kind of commercial rivalry with a Devon farmer needed every single wit the good Lord had given him.

So – yes – a trip to Barnstaple was quite an event. So was a trip in the other direction to Lynton, in its way. Not as big of course; Lynton was unable to match Barnstaple's range of shops.

But it had a post office, two grocers, a butcher's, a splendid sheepskin tailor's (not just a ready-made sales emporium; I mean a tailor's), an impressive town hall, a bank, a well-stocked art materials shop, a haberdasher's, dairy, fish-and-chip shop, and an Aladdin's cave (very appropriate for a business which sold lamps and paraffin heaters) of an ironmonger's which sold abso-lutely everything. Sweet shops (one cannily sited right outside the primary school) and a newsagent-cum-stationer-cum-card-shop-cum-toy-shop-cum-souvenir-emporium-cum-practically-ev-erything else. On the steep hill leading down to the fish-and-chip shop there was even a gents' outfitters. To say nothing of pubs (for the locals) and hotels (for the visitors).

Lynton received its fair share of those, because of its proximity to the more patronised resort of Lynmouth at the bottom of the hill, and because of the cliff railway which had been built by a publisher benefactor at the turn of the 19th/20th centuries. So there was no shortage of tea places and restaurants either.

This list of possible attractions is far from exhaustive. My range was circumscribed, naturally, by time, funds, and interests. And I had no motor car – well, not in the early days. Devon is pretty well supplied by rural bus routes (though far from sufficient for those who write grumpy letters to the local paper and to their MP). It needed to be; it is a big county. I understand that the Council's bill for providing school transport is one of the largest in the land.

So you couldn't go everywhere.

Secondly, even if I had had a car right from the start, and an elastic bank balance, there were many activities on offer which I did not pursue because I simply wasn't interested.

Anything to do with horses, for a start. I have never been astride a horse, and I do not regard it as any kind of deprivation. Rather relief. So not for me the crisp exhilaration of a dawn canter over the Moor. Not for me the saddle-bouncing and the high white cravat and the stirrup cup. Not for me the slavering hounds at the kill, and the hunt balls with the double-barrels and bare shoulders and nicknames which all seem to end in '-ie'.

The nearest I have come to anything equine is a nervous pat on the long, nostril-flared nose. The loss is quite probably mine, because I know full well that few animals can inspire so much attention, interest, devotion, and investment.

Another national passion which has passed me by, from infancy, is the 'seaside'. Growing up in London and, later, the suburbs before, during, and just after the War decreed that holidays – such as they were – meant the English coast. Sand, shingle, seaweed, rock, and mud. Well, OK, if that was your taste. It wasn't mine. I couldn't swim; I didn't like rock much (the sweet type, not the geological type); and I cringed at the awful hats with 'Kiss me quick' stuck on them. I must have been a rather odd child.

I went, because everybody did, but I certainly didn't live for it. The only activity I remember that absorbed me was standing at the water's edge and trying to work out how many times I could cause a pebble to bounce as I skimmed it across the surface. (I wonder if Barnes Wallis had done that when he was a child?)

Devon had all this to offer – and more – and still has. But you couldn't do everything. And, as I have been trying to explain, I wasn't in Devon for that. I was in Devon because of New Mill.

In answer to your question, then – what was I doing there?' – change, independence, a project, Barnstaple, Lynton, and of course, as I just said, New Mill.

But we are all human; even the ideal can pall sometimes. Devon had a way of dealing with that.

Exmoor pony

8

Exploring

If you wanted to get away from New Mill, and you had had enough of Barnstaple shops and upholstered buses for a while, there was always the hard way: putting on your walking boots and going to see Devon for yourself.

New Mill was/is on the edge of Exmoor, one of the last wildernesses in England. There are three down in the South-West – Exmoor, Dartmoor, and Bodmin Moor. Dartmoor is far and away the biggest, and to many the starkest. This may be because of the association of it in the public mind with the notorious prison. Just as people used to think of Ulster as a place where terrorist ambushes and bombs lurked round every corner, so we are tempted to imagine Dartmoor as the permanent haunt and hiding place of a constant stream of wild-looking escapees with jutting jaws, five-day stubble, and arrows all over their clothes. As with all clichés, it is a truth long buried in ignorance, over-simplification, and habit. We like the cliché; it is almost comforting. Throw in the Hound of the Baskervilles, and you have an almost immovable pre-conception.

Bodmin is not so well known, though Daphne du Maurier and *Jamaica Inn* make a fair cliché challenge. I have been there only twice, and it is indeed an unfeeling place, more likely to give you a chill than, I felt, Dartmoor. My impression is that far fewer tourists walk or ride on Bodmin. Bodmin is simply not so embedded in the national subconscious as Exmoor and Dartmoor.

Exmoor is not to be outdone in the literary stakes. Dartmoor has Sherlock Holmes and the Hound; Bodmin has Mary Yellan and smugglers at the inn; Exmoor has the semi-outlaw Doones – *Lorna*

Doone to be precise. Not so high up the popularity list now as the Hound and Mary, but very popular in its day, and still exploited, naturally, in the constant campaign to attract tourists.

I have no logical evidence to back up my hunch, but to me Exmoor is somehow more intimate and manageable than the other two. It is not so threatening – though I am sure that, if you were careless enough, you could die of exposure on all three.

Perhaps the simple truth is that I came across Exmoor first. I was seven years old. I was an evacuee, a London boy bemused by 'the country'. I never went up on Exmoor in the eight months I was at Swimbridge (I never even went to South Molton), but somehow it worked its way into the subconscious, and remained there long afterwards – over twenty years. When the chance came to spend time there, I found myself responding without much conscious thought. As I have explained, I was without the funds, resources, knowledge, and experience to feel confident about making something of it, but I simply wanted to get started.

So – what happened when I at last got around to having a look at it?

If you examine the Ordnance Survey Map of North Devon – or the more lush tourist dressed-up maps that they put out today – you will see Exmoor marked as the 'Exmoor National Park'. Well, it used to be 'Exmoor Forest' on my old map. So if you had never visited before, you could have been forgiven for expecting a sort of windblown, granite-strewn Wild Wood.

Not so. That is not what 'forest' originally meant. Many a visitor to the New Forest in Hampshire may have begun to get a glimmering of the puzzle by visiting it and finding a great deal of open space. Well, it's the same with Exmoor – in fact, even more open space per square mile. Though *in toto* it's not very big actually – only about thirty miles across.

So – why 'forest'?

'Forest' is one of those semi-technical terms which have a much more common meaning for the majority of people who come across it. It is a very good example of the fact that the most deceptive words in the language are often not the long and complicated ones, but the simple ones. Everyone knows what a forest is. Or they think they do. They have sat through many a childhood story in which the hero or heroine is lost, or cast away, or abandoned, in a huge, terrifying wilderness crowded, overhung, and dominated by thousands of menacing, twisted tree trunks with the wind howling hellishly in their branches and their boles leering like devilish faces.

I repeat, that is not what 'forest' originally meant. To find out we must go right back.

We are used to the idea that the whole of England is lived in. Which may sound a bit stupid: of course it's lived in; it is a tiny island and there are sixty million of us.

But it wasn't always like that. In the eleventh century, round about the time of the Norman Conquest, the figure would have been only three per cent of that. We had no censuses then, obviously, but the historians and cartographers and demographic analysts tell us that their best guess at the population is about two million, if that. Only three per cent.

Life then was hard, very hard. For the vast majority of people it was unremitting struggle with the land to make it produce enough food to sustain life. There were only twenty-four hours in the day, and there were few tools. Fewer gadgets. Fewer still machines. There was a limit to the land that you actually farmed, because you hadn't the time, resources, or energy to farm any more. It was a long time before circumstances allowed farmers to think of a cash crop.

So, if you had a village, the amount of land that was farmed stretched only a few furlongs (furrow-longs) in any direction. Beyond that the land might be heath, moor, marsh, downland, anything. If it was fertile, it would have been overgrown with the natural vegetation of a temperate climate (which is where England lay) – deciduous forest.

But all this land was not called 'forest'; it was called 'waste', because nobody had a use for it – beyond scavenging or gleaning for berries, kindling, acorns, and so on. England was not dotted with close clusters of villages; remember, for every hundred people today there would have been three then. Hamlets, villages, any settlements would have been spaced out. So you could have travelled for miles without seeing a ploughed field. Just as England strikes an American visitor today as 'small', so medieval England would have struck a modern time traveller as 'empty'.

Which still does not explain 'forest'.

Ordinary people tended to have a very largely vegetarian diet. Rulers – knights, noblemen, thegns, barons, dukes, princes, kings – aspired to something they thought was better. Meat. And it was all there for the taking – if you had the time, the money, and the resources. England teemed with wild animals. Not just the small ones we see today – hedgehogs, squirrels, foxes, rabbits (relatively late arrivals, introduced, we think, by the Normans themselves), otters, badgers – but hefty ones – roe deer, fallow deer, red deer, wild boar, even wolves and bears.

So all those knights, noblemen, thegns, barons, dukes, princes, and kings hunted. To do that, they needed space. Space for riding and chasing (which was as exciting as the catch and the kill – probably more so), but also for the animals themselves. If they did not have space and cover to live and breed, there would be no more hunting.

No huntsman wanted barns and ditches and cornstalks and flocks of sheep getting in the way, so land was set aside for hunting. Forcibly cleared if necessary. It was outside the normal tracks and farming strips of the village. And that's what 'forest' means: it comes from the Latin '*foras*', which means 'outside'. Well, that's what my Latin dictionary says.

Because it could be anywhere in the countryside – according to the nobleman's tastes, property, and resources – it could be anything: trees of course (real forest), or heath, moor, downland, even perhaps pasture, and so on.

A prince or a king, or anybody with the land and the authority, could simply declare that such and such a piece of land was to be set aside as a hunting preserve. It became his 'forest'. And you could only kill animals there if you were the prince or king in question or his friends and family. Which was why Robin Hood and his merry men were always in such trouble; they were technically thieves, because a man who owned a piece of land owned any living animal on it.

So a piece of land did not have to be covered with trees. Hence the open spaces of Exmoor. Indeed, actual trees were so rare in some areas of the Moor that there is one which is actually marked individually on the Ordnance Survey map – the 'Hoar Oak tree'. So – the Exmoor Forest – we have got there in the end.

The Moor is still being fought over. Not, as it once was, between lords and poachers, but between the various 'interests' which reckon that they have a claim on it. The owners, naturally. Every square inch of England – however wild – has an owner. Then there are the farmers who have land bordering on it, and who have a furtive habit of taking nibbles out of it. If left alone, they would have the Moor down to pasture and ploughland in no time at all. So, thirdly, there are the conservationists, who campaign constantly to stop them, or at least to restrict them, or hold them up. Most recently, we have had a fourth group – the developers, who want to 'make something' of Exmoor – be it holiday caravan village, activity centre, even (I once heard) race track. Rich, powerful, and persistent. And they call out nearly everybody to stop them – farmers, fishermen, walkers, ordinary inhabitants, and of course conservationists. It's never-ending.

I am sure an expert would spot tell-tale signs of his particular interest wherever he went, but, if you were an ordinary ignorant member of the public (or a newly-arrived townee living in an old cottage), you would not get a whiff of this controversy when you ventured up there. I say 'up' (a Devonian would say 'up auver') because the highest point, Dunkery Beacon, is 519 metres high (1,730 feet). Hoar Oak Hill is 437 metres (1577 feet). If you left New Mill to go up to, say, Woodbarrow, it was a pretty steady climb all the way.

You would have the whole of North Devon to yourself. You could see Wales one way and Dartmoor the other. Lundy Island out to the west, and maybe Dunkery to the east. Of course you were not the only walker, but you would never find the human race imposing on you. Those you did meet were usually doing the same thing as you, so you had a joint interest, and conversations were amiable affairs, without a nibbling farmer or a race-track builder in sight.

You would never be short of variety. On a good autumn or spring day, you could walk in shirt-sleeves; in the middle of August you could be hunched against driving rain like stair rods. The weather could change violently, and quickly, within a single day. Anybody who ventures there without a good sweater and a sound waterproof is asking for the trouble he gets.

The wind is with you most of the time. This can produce bewildering changes in the skies – billowing white, lowering greys, great wisps of cloud speeding across like Concord. I read somewhere that John Constable (he of *The Hay Wain*) liked to make lightning water-colour sketches of striking patterns of clouds because he knew he had only a short time to enjoy them, and they would never return again – well, not quite like that. I believe he used to refer to them as 'my skies'. Well, he would have been in his seventh heaven up on the Moor.

There were a good many signposts, but you would have been ill-advised to go without a map. Tracks had a nasty habit of changing, or even of disappearing altogether. So there was nothing for it but a compass bearing, or an eye fixed on a distant 'sight', or memory, common sense, and luck.

You needed to keep your eyes open not only for where you were going, and for where you had been, but for what was right under your feet. Some grass, naturally, but not much. Mostly heather. Gorse – that was easy to spot. What was not easy was the wet bits. If you looked ahead – always a good idea – you would catch sight of a patch of some green which was greener than natural. This was the notorious sphagnum moss. It looked lovely and mossy and comfortable from close above, but step on it and you could be up to the hocks, and often much higher, in a bog.

One does not hear these days of people dying in a bog, but, then, if you were alone when it happened, the nature of your demise would be unlikely to be reported. I have no doubt that there were a few casualties in past years (hence the 'Farmer Mole' legend). Arthur Conan Doyle, in *The Hound of the Baskervilles,* would have us believe that Dartmoor ponies could die in the awful Grimpen Mire, so I suppose Exmoor ponies could have met the same fate.

So, legend or no legend, bottomless bogs or no bottomless bogs, it behoved you to exercise reasonable vigilance and common sense.

Water, as opposed to mud and bog, was a much less tiresome hazard. Streams were rarely more than a foot or two deep (in good weather, that is), and the worst you could get as a rule was wet feet. Some rivers drained to the south. The place called Exehead is self-explanatory. I have seen the very spot where the River Barle comes out of the ground, at a corner of Pinkworthy Pond (pronounced 'Pinkery'). To the north flowed the system of streams and rivers which joined at Lynmouth.

They tend not to call them 'streams' on Exmoor; they are 'waters'. Ilkerton Water, Oare Water, Badgworthy ('Badgery') Water, Hoar Oak Water, and so on. Near the mouth of Badgworthy is the village of Oare, in whose church Lorna Doone was shot on her wedding day.

They are all a feast for the eyes, therapy for the ears, and inspiration for the would-be poet and painter. Gorse and sedge, hazel and birch, couch grass and heather. Hedges with their upper ends bent over almost at ninety degrees by the ever-blowing wind. Rocks and stones creating a non-stop symphony of rippling sound as the water trickles, bounces, rushes, or cascades over them. Purples and browns and greens in endless variations and nuances. In the autumn the fallen leaves display a cornucopia of russets, rusts, ochres, siennas, and near-blacks which would be a challenge to any artist.

It is all very good for you.

After what I have said, I hope you will appreciate that, even if you are up there alone, it is not empty; there is so much to look at. And not only Nature; there are marks of man too. There is the great monolith, lonely and threatening when you get close to it – the Long Stone. If only we knew how, and why, that got there.

There is the Fortescue Memorial, beside the road between South Molton and Simonsbath (pronounced not 'Simonsbath' but 'Simmonsbath'). It was put there by Winifred, the wife of Sir John Fortescue, whose claim to fame is the authorship of a monumental History of the British Army. The Fortescues are a powerful, and very prolific, Exmoor noble family. The family tree, which goes back to the Norman Conquest, is sprinkled with knights and earls. Some of the family still live near the Moor, at Castle Hill just outside Filleigh, and have a great deal of local clout.

One more example, and then I'll let you alone.

Another influential Devon family were the Aclands. On the Moor stands a hut, built for shelter against the capricious weather. It was built as a memorial to Sir Thomas Dyke Acland, who lived from 1787 to 1871. It bears the following tribute from a loving and grateful family:

'In remembrance of the father who, during more than fifty years, took Sunday walks up this combe with his children and grandchildren, training them in the love of nature and of Christian poetry, this Wind and Weather Hut was built.'

I think that is absolutely perfect.

Rather more prosaically, Sir Thomas left another legacy which is with us still, though very few people know what it is. So I'll tell you.

In the middle of the nineteenth century, there were no public exams for secondary age children, for the simple reason that there was no such thing as a secondary education system. There were the university degree exams, but that was about that. In the 1850's, four men, all associated with Devon, set about remedying the situation. The fruit of their work was the very first public exams for children of secondary age – the Oxford and Cambridge Local Examinations. They began in 1858, and they were the direct ancestor of GCSE today. One of those four men was Earl Fortescue (of the above family). The second was the Revd. Joseph Lloyd Brereton, vicar of the village of West Buckland, near Fortescue's Filleigh. He also, along with Earl Fortescue, founded the very first secondary school dedicated to the education of the 'middle classes', and he set it up at West Buckland. The third was Frederick Temple, who became Bishop of Exeter (and later Archbishop of Canterbury). The fourth was Sir Thomas Dyke Acland.

It seems remarkable to me that these great strides in education were made by four men who lived and worked in what fashionable England at the time would have called the back of beyond.

One could go on. There is something more-ish about Exmoor.

9

Meeting

The company was more-ish too. I have been at pains to show what an isolated place New Mill was – a solitary place in a remote valley at the edge of a bleak moor in a remote, lowly-populated rural county. A reader could be forgiven for concluding that one lived a Robinson Crusoe sort of life. I did indeed liken part of that life to the existence our Mr. Crusoe endured in many respects.

However, that was mainly to do with improvisation and making do. There were other respects too.

For instance, New Mill was in fact not completely solitary. There was a guest-house and riding stables at one end of the valley, out of sight indeed, but only about a quarter of a mile away; and at the top of New Mill Lane there was New Mill Farm. Opposite the cottage, across the stream and up the hill, lay East Ilkerton Farm, about a kilometre away as the crow, and, presumably, other feathered species, flew. Also out of sight. That was the point: they were there, but you couldn't see them. So, when you gazed out of your bedroom window, it looked as if you had Devon to yourself. And, as the vast majority of people live either next door to somebody else or a stone's throw away from them, one can feel justified in using the adjective 'solitary'. Most houses are together; New Mill wasn't.

There were plenty of other valleys like ours too. We did not have a monopoly on remote valleys. Indeed one could argue that the whole of North Devon is made up of remote valleys. It was those steep, remote valleys which had produced the Lynmouth Flood.

Exmoor wasn't bleak either – well, not all the time. Exmoor was rather like the little girl with the curl on the top of her forehead:

when it was good it was very, very good, but when it was bad it was horrid. The fact remained that, when I came back from a stay in New Mill, I usually had some kind of tan. At any rate you would have known that I had been outdoors.

However, Devon was unquestionably a rural county. And a remote one. Stuck out at the end of England, open to the winds and storms of the English Channel, the Bristol Channel, the Irish Sea, and the Atlantic. Devonians of course think it is the centre of the universe, and can not understand why the rest of Britain think of it as so distant and so behind beyond. Londoners may talk of going 'down' to Devon, but Devonians also talk of going 'done Lunnon'. (I should imagine the situation is more extreme in the case of Cornwall, where they talk of 'going up into England'.)

Readers may also have gathered the impression that I never saw anybody. That impression too needs modifying. In fact I got to know a surprising range of people, considering the position of New Mill, and considering the relatively low population density of Devon.

It's common sense if you stop to think about it. The fewer people you meet, the greater attention you are likely to give them. We are all, or nearly all, social animals. So, when you meet them, you are more likely to talk.

For instance, I found out that Joe, the postman, who regularly walked all the way down New Mill Lane to deliver my letters, ran a one-man taxi service in his spare time. I knew that three or four sons of the local builder were in the volunteer fire brigade. I discovered that a man who lived in a row of houses just a little way up the hill out of Barbrook ran a hair-cutting service in his sitting room. I was told that the TV comedian Dave Allen had a house near Lynton – Martinhoe I think it was. I met him later in a Lynton garage repair shop. Smaller than I had imagined (he was, not the repair shop). Perhaps it was that high chair that made him look bigger. (Perhaps that was why he used it.)

I wasn't living there, remember. (That came later.) I picked up these nuggets of information during holiday visits. And I didn't get about much because I didn't have a car. It's odd then, isn't it? The further you are from people, and the fewer they are, the better you can get to know them.

I can see Fred Leworthy now. Ken introduced me to him soon after I arrived. If you remember – and I'll tell you again if you don't – he was the man from whom Ken bought New Mill in the first place. He it was who, suddenly presented with a prospective buyer for a dilapidated property that had not been occupied for over a decade, and which he had not thought was worth caring for – like Everest, it was just 'there' – had the presence of mind, and the commercial instinct, to reply to Ken's offer of £500, instantly, with 'seven hundred and fifty'.

He must have been taking a chance. Ken could easily have walked away from an owner who had upped his offer by fifty per cent, and Fred would have been stuck with waiting for another decade to turn his ruin into money. Perhaps he had read his buyer correctly, and sensed he was good for a little more – fifty per cent more to be precise.

Certainly there were no flies on our Fred. The screwed-up eyes told you that. He had a presence too. That is why I can still remember him so clearly, and I don't suppose I met him more than a dozen times all told.

He was not a big man, not like his son John, whom I met later. If you had had to produce a picture of a typical shrewd Devon farmer, you would have come up with Fred. If you had to paint a picture of Fred, you would have used a lot of primary colours. There was nothing neutral about him. His clothes proclaimed what he was the minute you saw him – from the cap which lived on his head to the leather gaiters and boots.

He had a rich accent – naturally. It was evident in the stories which littered his conversation. That conversation, which he enjoyed, and which he was very good at, was enhanced by a choice of vocabulary which you would not normally have attributed to a man who spent the vast majority of his time out of doors, and had almost certainly left school at the earliest opportunity.

He was emphatic, I remember, about the deleterious effects of too much air. He had known two young parents who were apparently obsessional about 'fresh urr'. He had marvelled at the way they exposed their infant to wind and cold without covering his head. He shook his head. ' 'Twas always the same - 'e got to 'ave fresh urr.' Fred was convinced that no good would come of it. Indeed, no good did, but at this distance of time I forget what this 'no good' was – but it was pretty dire.

Of course I didn't know him well in the sense that I knew what his likes and dislikes were, how good a father and husband he was (his son was a gentle, slow-speaking, amiable man and his wife was a lovely lady), how he spent his leisure time (if he had any), and what other people thought of him. But those primary colours made him memorable. Despite what I have just said, you felt that you *did* know him.

His son John, for all his retiring manner, could spring surprises. He had his ration of Devon sharpness and deliberation. One day a contractor unloaded a truckful of muck in John's farmyard and knocked on his door to ask for payment. A dispute arose; the man claimed more than John said he had agreed beforehand. The contractor got cross and uttered dark threats about bringing pressure to bear. John shrugged and said, 'Well, you 'ad better way pick 'n up and put 'n back on the truck, cos I ain't payin'.'

John and his wife Kath were good neighbours. John had a telephone, which New Mill didn't, and that got me, and later us, out of one or two awkward situations. Their first son was born round about the same time as our son Stephen. We had little in common but neighbourliness, but that served us very well.

The same could be said of John's cousin David. We didn't see a lot of each other, and we differed in almost every way, but he was a good neighbour. There was nothing he could not fix, mend, arrange, remove, carry, deliver, or otherwise bring about. He was a big man. Tall, as I said, like John. But he would have made two of John. Another man with a presence, like his uncle. The horse he rode – and he was fond of riding – was enormous. It needed to be.

84

He hunted, naturally.

He had been born and raised in a farm way out in the wilds of Exmoor. If you thought New Mill was solitary, you should have seen Shallowford. The family must have seen few people, and I would venture to suggest that David had not been the best attender at school. So he had an accent all his own; for six months I could not understand a thing he said.

He had married a girl from London (or Essex, I forget which). It must have been a major culture shock for both of them. With such linguistic barriers between them, the animal magnetism between them must have been of a very high voltage to help them sustain the first year or two of marriage. They had two children, inevitably, one of each. The girl was a dear; the boy, from the look of him, would have made a notable impression on the local primary school; there were no tell-tale bulges between his shoulders to indicate the presence of wings.

David, like John, simply accepted me – and, later, my wife and children. He was not pushy; he was not wary; not stand-offish, obstructive, unhelpful, not negative in any way. He was just, for a while anyway, impenetrable.

His wife Maureen did us favours too. For all that she had been whirled from an urban society to a rural one, she looked well able to take care of herself. She learned to make some pretty mean Devonshire cream – not as easy as one might think. David, I'm sure, was not the easiest of people to live with. He had his likes and dislikes; he had his regular habits; he had his values; and he, like everyone else, had his faults. But Maureen never showed any sign of diffidence about her capacity to handle him.

They lived in a small row of cottages up beside Caffyn's Cross, on the side of the main road opposite the disused railway bridge. In fact, they were called Caffyn's Cottages.

One of their neighbours was a maiden lady who had been a nurse and health visitor, and who had retired there a few years before. Miss Blackmore prided herself on her Devonshire associations. Well, with a name like Blackmore, she would, wouldn't she? I forget the exact detail of her family connection with R.D. Blackmore, the author of *Lorna Doone*, but it was there all right. She didn't go on about it, but she took care to make you acquainted with it. She spoke beautifully, and my guess would be that, if pressed, she would have described herself as 'coming from a good family'. Where this family lived I can't remember, but it was clearly important in her life. She had two sisters, also maiden ladies, whom we later met.

Like many maiden ladies who had joined a dignified profession and who had fended for themselves all their lives, she was of an independent turn of mind, and had some pretty set views about a lot of things. She would not have central heating, for instance. She always had an open fire, and her sitting room was cosy and welcoming. Not so when she later inherited a much bigger house in Parracombe, a few miles up the road. It was like Ice Station Zebra. We didn't visit very often, but, when we did, we came away with blue noses and fingers.

This inheritance raised a question which we never really answered. As I said, she never corrected an impression she may have created that she was 'of good family'. That is, with 'property'. She claimed ownership of another house along the road between Lynton and Parracombe, and, for all I remember, there may have been others. But she never lived with the slightest ostentation. Her wardrobe, for instance, would have been covered completely by the adjectives grey, brown, and black. Any kind of reference to the concept of fashion would never have got near her dictionary. She ran a car, a typical spinster's car. She never dined out, or, if she did, she never referred to it.

She went on Spartan holidays. One I remember was an odyssey to the Middle East. She joined a group (of similar stalwarts, presumably), who got on a charabanc in Kingston upon Thames and were taken to India – all the way. It was proudly named 'The East Indiaman'. She told us that they had been warned about the dodgy meat on parts of the journey, so she was taking a huge joint of it, wrapped up in sacking. Sacking! A health visitor – sacking!

She did not believe in refrigerators. 'Unhealthy,' she said. Which was odd, coming from a health visitor. She did not smoke, naturally. I don't remember seeing her with a glass of 'drink' in her hand.

But she was fit. My word, she was fit. Like Queen Victoria, who froze her personal servants by her indifference to the cold in Buckingham Palace, Miss Blackmore simply did not notice the low temperatures in her house at Parracombe. Even when we went to visit her, some time after we had left New Mill, she did not gee up the fire; indeed, I'm not sure she had a fire at all. She had a pile of logs outside too, but she did not deem it cold enough to have to use it. It was not because of bad manners. You could never accuse her of that. She came of 'good family', remember? She knew what was correct, and always did it. She saw to it that we were well fed and watered, but warm? No. She was warm, and always had been, and assumed that a young family, being healthy like her, was warm too.

One result of this was that she had no qualms about facing the great outdoors. I have already referred to her coach trip on the East Indiaman. And there were others. No quiet hours for her, knitting with a shawl round her shoulders, and 'enjoying her retirement'. She was capable of knocking off the miles on foot too. She was well acquainted with the outstanding features of the Moor, and, if memory serves, once accompanied us on a trek to the Longstone. I need hardly mention the tweed skirts, robust overcoats, knitted stockings, and strong, 'sensible' shoes.

Like Fred, she was completely at ease with the person she was. She had long since accepted her spinster status, and, so far as we could tell, did not resent a single thing that had happened to her – or not happened, as the case may be. A trifle eccentric, maybe, and with her share of prejudices and illogicalities, but strong, definite, and capable. If you had wanted somebody comforting beside you in a revolution, you could have done a lot worse than choose Miss Blackmore.

You knew where you were with Miss Blackmore. And it remained 'Miss Blackmore' all the time we knew her. We knew her Christian name – Dorothy – but we would never have dreamed of using it. The boys were always the soul of courtesy in their dealings with her, without any coaching from us. They too would never have dreamed of being anything but totally formal and correct. Even when they referred to her out of her presence, it was always 'Miss Blackmore'. Incidentally, she never used our Christian names either – not directly, face to face.

Because of this correctness and propriety of her background, it was going to be no surprise that she should strike up an acquaintance with Ken. She was 'good family'; he was public school.

Shortly after she had retired, she had acquired a dog, for the usual reasons of company and security. A Labrador. A lovely golden brown colour. He was fully grown by the time we got to know hm. Hefty. Moved like an all-in wrestler. Friendly and genial, with an active tail. Though I wouldn't have liked to be in the shoes of an intruder he had taken a dislike to.

Miss Blackmore was in the habit of bringing Wally (that was his name – Wally) down New Mill Lane on a Sunday morning. It was perfect exercise for him, with the added bonus of a splash in the stream.

So Ken too evolved the habit of giving her a cup of tea and a chocolate biscuit (or, as he was fond of joking, a 'choccy bikky'). When I joined the New Mill *ménage*, I was absorbed into this ritual. And ritual it was. Ken and I always made sure that, whatever job we were doing, we could have it at the stage whereat we were able to leave it in order to play host.

This continued after I had acquired a family. Of course Ken was there only during the holidays, but, after we had made the decision to leave Kingston and 'go native', we were there all the time. Miss Blackmore enjoyed the company of a person like Ken, from a background similar to her own, but she liked family company too. Being a health visitor had no doubt made her fluent in a wide variety of human situations, and I think she looked forward to her Sunday mornings.

She was very kind too when my wife was in the later stages of her pregnancy with our son Stephen, as I said. There was no telephone in New Mill, and Lynton Cottage Hospital was a few miles away. So she invited Mrs. Coates to spend her afternoons in her house, till I got home from Barnstaple. For a woman in those circumstances, there were few more reassuring people to have round you than a health visitor. We did not take advantage of her hospitality every single weekday, but it was a generous offer, and we were grateful. It reinforces my point about having Miss Blackmore at your side in a revolution. I have little doubt that, if the situation had arisen, Miss Blackmore could have delivered the child herself.

A lot of people might have been tempted, on a slight acquaintance, to label her as 'formidable'. And with a good deal of evidence. We saw the kind side too, but could well understand why she would have appeared like that. However, if you wanted through-and-through formidability, you should have seen sister Miriam. Also unmarried, independent, and downright. She visited Dorothy once or twice and we met her. When we heard that Miriam was *not* going to retire to Barbrook, I won't say we heaved a sigh of relief, but we had had just the slightest of qualms at the prospect of having two Misses Blackmore in the offing.

And there was a third. Sister Florrie came to live with Dorothy. We met her too. But she was a completely different prospect. Quiet, overweight, unathletic, possibly ill, and self-effacing. With two such masterful sisters, we often wondered what sort of life Florrie had had. It was odd that she was not known as 'Florence'. You would have thought, with their background and character, Miriam and Dorothy would have at least said 'Florence' when they were referring to her with other people, but they didn't. There might be a clue there. She didn't stay long – moved away again. I don't know why and I don't know where she went. I don't think she lived very much longer. All rather sad.

Dorothy herself moved away in the end, to her other house in Parracombe. This was some time after we too had moved from New Mill to a house just outside Barnstaple.

We did not visit her as often as we should have done, but, when we did, there was no resentment, no change whatever in her attitude. The house was just as cold, and the welcome was just as warm. We brought her to our house too, and she enjoyed that just as much. She made the trip to Barnstaple to attend my mother's funeral. (They had met some years before when my mother and stepfather lived for a few months in New Mill [long story]. They were of an age, they had similarities of personality, and they got along fine.)

One day, without any warning, she collapsed in her kitchen. The doctor said later that she could well have been dead before she hit the floor. She was ninety years old.

10

Researching

'Where do I come from?'

We all get curious sooner or later about who we are and how we got here. By the same token, if you stay any length of time in a place, you get curious not only about who you are but *where* you are. You start to ask questions. You start searching. This was the more likely in my case because New Mill represented a life so different from the one I was leading in Kingston. Indeed, different from the one I had led since the very beginning. I was born in Shoreditch (Bow Bells country), and had spent nearly all my life in built-up areas – apart from National Service in Kenya.

True, I had spent eight months in North Devon as an evacuee, but believe me, when you are seven years old and alone in a 'foreign' place, you don't see or find out much. I never went as far as South Molton, only five miles away. I don't remember seeing any other thoroughfare except the lane through which I walked to school and the road beside which the school actually stood.

I walked that lane four times every school day (I went 'home' for lunch), and that was about that. Oh yes – there were a few little excursions with my friend Bernard Simmons, another evacuee, but I don't think they lasted very long and we didn't go anywhere really adventurous. To be honest, my only clear recollection is of somewhere near a stream, and there were kingcups nearby. I had never seen kingcups before. But I do remember Bernard's hoop – a lusty iron affair as big as a grown-up bicycle wheel, which he propelled with some kind of bamboo stick, and which accompanied him everywhere. Kids today have little skateboards; Bernard had his hoop and his stick.

He came from Chelsea (that is the name that sticks in the memory), and so was one of that army of worldly London kids who descended upon the unsuspecting denizens of the quiet countryside and made a considerable impact – with their colourful language, sharp wits, disdain for authority, smelly underclothes (or no underclothes at all), and refusal to be overawed by anything. It was only nimby-pimbies like me who got bullied. Bernard and his mates could give as good as they got – with interest.

How I came to be involved with him is a mystery; we could not have been more different. A little illustration will show just how different. Bernard liked to sing a song which was clearly common fare among his own fellow-delinquents in London. I had never heard it before (which shows you how unworldly I was). It was called *My Old Man's a Dustman*. It became a hit in the 1960's when Lonnie Donegan made it a regular item in his skiffle concert repertoire, but my guess is that it has slipped back into obscurity again.

Lonnie cleaned up the words a bit, but Bernard had used the unexpurgated version, some of which was barely intelligible to me. I certainly would never have dreamed of using them myself, because I hardly knew what they meant.

But what really struck me was the fact that the composition was so poor. The tune was flat and bare; the rhythm seemed repetitive; the vulgarity (which came later), the cheeky concept, all made no impact. I could see no virtue in it. The first two lines went something like this:

'My old man's dustman; he wears a dustman's hat.

He shot five 'undred Jerries, and what d'you think of those?'

Well, that's what Bernard sang.

'But Bernard,' I said, 'it doesn't rhyme.'

I was an aesthete at seven. Bernard could not even have pronounced the word 'aesthete', much less have understood what it meant. Neither could I, at seven. But I was sufficiently aware to appreciate the point, even if I could not put such a name to it.

How *did* we come to gravitate together? What on earth did we see in each other?

So – yes – I knew a little about Devon, a very little. But that was a foot in the door. Now that I had 'property' there, I needed to push a little.

I was a historian, so I jolly well *ought* to find out something about my new county. And Devon was, as I said, so different that common sense dictated that there ought to be something really worth learning about. If not, what the hell was I doing there?

This was where Ken came in. For a short time, while we were making my half of the house habitable, we shared a meal table; and for some time after that, whenever he was down for the holidays, we shared tea and coffee breaks, not to mention our Sunday salon with Miss Blackmore. Miss Blackmore knew a thing or two as well, so between them they introduced me to a good deal of Devon lore.

Do you remember the first evening that Mole spent in Rat's house after he had left his own on that magical spring morning? The Rat 'told him river stories till suppertime'. As I picked up all these titbits of local knowledge, I felt a little bit like Mole.

Incidentally, I looked up the reference in Chapter One of *The Wind in the Willows*, just to make sure, and came across another relevant sentence lower down. The Mole, it said, 'entered into the joy of running water'. Well, I did that too.

Perhaps the most obvious feature to note about our surroundings was the railway. The bridge is the very first thing you see when you get off the bus at Caffyn's Cross. You didn't have to be Sherlock Holmes to deduce that a railway had once run underneath it.

It had a little rise in the middle, presumably to accommodate the engine funnel. Or perhaps they built all local bridges like this for reasons which are way beyond the understanding of anybody outside the engineering profession. Anyway, it didn't take a great deal of imagination to picture oneself standing in the middle of the bridge, hearing the rattle and chuff, and being brushed by two plumes of smut-filled smoke as the engine puffed underneath. Long ago, small boys used to do it above railway lines all over the country.

It was a narrow-gauge line, and the train had very few carriages. It ran from Lynton to Barnstaple, and was the brain-child of George Newnes, a successful London publisher, who had taken a fancy to the area. (More of him later.) It opened in 1898, and ran for thirty-seven years. It had its loyal band of regular users. I have spoken to a lady who used to attend Barnstaple Grammar School from Lynton. She said it was often a bit of a rush up the hill to the station. (This had to be up above the town, because there was no way a railway line could cope with the gradient from the hill down to the level of the town in the distance available. Indeed, the old coach road, they said, was so steep that passengers had to get out and push, to ease the strain on the poor horses.)

It was a problem which has presented itself to every school child since secondary schools were invented: how do you get from a late breakfast-table to the bus or the train – in time? But the Lynton-Barnstaple line catered for that. The guard would see the regulars panting up the road, with satchels swinging and banging on hips and a piece of cold toast clamped between the front teeth, and he would hold the train for them. The friendly line.

From Lynton the train passed through stations with names out of the world of Beatrix Potter and Kenneth Grahame – Caffyn's Halt, Woody Bay, Parracombe Halt, Blackmoor Gate, Snapper, Bratton Fleming, down to Pilton and Barnstaple (which at one time had four stations).

Another story about the line concerns the local rector, the Revd. John Chanter. You met him in Chapter Six. Chanter was in the habit of riding on the line, naturally, and was inspired to institute a regular practice, which he maintained for many years. He would carry with him packets of the seeds of wild flowers. These he would broadcast out of the train window as they chugged through the cuttings or rattled across the embankments. I believe the profusion of wild flowers beside the line is still referred to in the guide-books.

The line became the victim of progress – of course. This time nemesis came in the shape of the internal combustion engine. Another engine. More flexible, more available, and more private.

Inevitably, a legion of local enthusiasts rallied to preserve the railway. Only a hundred years before, local worthies had banded together to *prevent* the railways desecrating the countryside; now they were gathering to keep them open. Like the first noble protest, it was a lost cause. A final, last-ditch protest meeting was scheduled at Barnstaple in the late summer of 1935. Nearly everybody who attended came in a motor car.

So the line died, and mouldered. One exception was at Lynton, where an enterprising buyer obtained the station buildings and part of the land bearing the line. That too gets into the guide books, because the new owner could now boast that he had the longest, narrowest garden in England.

The railway was not the only benefaction of Mr. Newnes. He built the town hall, for a start. I am no connoisseur of architecture, but it seems an individual, and not unpleasing, establishment to me. Unlike many prominent men who sought to perpetuate their own memory, he did not think on grandiose lines. After all, there is nothing particularly palatial about a narrow-gauge railway, or a town hall.

My guess is that he developed other facilities of the town because he invited his well-provided friends down to stay. No doubt a hotel or two owes its origin to his presence, and to that of his entourage. However, far and away his greatest monument is the famous cliff railway, which descended from Lynton straight down the cliff to Lynmouth. All done by the weight of water. It commands the attention, and once you have seen it, you have to make a date to go up it – or down it. If you want the engineering details, I have no doubt that a whole library of guidebooks can accommodate you. It has been a favourite with visitors since its inception.

However, I am given to understand that the population of Lynton has not grown all that much over the centuries. One Exmoor-lover, J.H.B. Peel, turned a generous compliment in his *Portrait of Exmoor*: 'Lynton's main street contains enough shops to create the substance of a town without destroying the spirit of a village.' [Robert Hale and Co., 1970, p. 74.]

All this, and more, I got from Ken and Miss Blackmore, which induced me to find out a little more for myself. It transpired that George Newnes was by no means the first national figure to have become involved with Lynton and Lynmouth.

In the eighteenth century, it was the habit of those with the wherewithal to travel widely in mainland Europe. Indeed, even before that, young noblemen did not regard their education complete until they had completed the Grand Tour – a youthful odyssey in which they overspent, over-indulged, and overcame a lot of their inhibitions, no doubt happily assisted by mentors, hoteliers, brothel-keepers, and con-men from the art world. However, at the end of the eighteenth century, the conquests of Napoleon and the near-constant war between England and France effectively shut off the continent for long periods, and men with money to spend began to look elsewhere – in England this time.

One of them, the poet Robert Southey, reached Lynton in 1799, and was so taken with it that he was moved to describe the area as 'England's Little Switzerland' – which did wonders for publicity. R.D. Blackmore became very well acquainted with the place, because he set *Lorna Doone* there. Wordsworth and Coleridge were taken with it enough to consider living there. The artist Gainsborough had anticipated them all by spending his honeymoon there, and was similarly bewitched – but then he probably had rose-tinted spectacles on at the time.

In 1812, another poet, Percy Shelley, (or, as all the books say, 'Percy Bysshe Shelley' – though I don't know why; was it like 'George Bernard Shaw'?) actually did go to live there, and used to invite his literary friends down. The internet will tell you that the list of celebrity visitors goes on: Henry James, Bertrand Russell, Henry Williamson, J.M. Barrie – everybody, it seems, except the Pope and the Beatles.

And that is not so far-fetched as one might imagine; I believe one of the Beatles bought a vast estate on Exmoor, though I have no idea how long he stayed there. I have yet to hear of property agents from the Vatican investigating the possibility of a moorland retreat for His Holiness.

So all these celebrities (and no doubt more that I don't know about) sang the praises of Exmoor and got it into the newspapers and the gossip columns. Benefactors like George Newnes did their best to improve it. But it was the Knights (John and his son Frederick) who set out to 'develop' it – with all the emotive implications that those inverted commas convey.

The Knights were ironmasters from Worcestershire, and they brought their business experience, knowhow, and profit motive to Exmoor. Their plan was to replace the heather of the high moor with farmland, and to exploit the resources under the ground by trying to set up a copper-mining industry. This is not the place to offer an economic history of North Devon in the nineteenth century, but take it from me it makes for interesting reading, and it's all there in the books, the internet, the libraries, and the learned magazines.

You can see the imprint of the Knights on Exmoor today, most of it above ground, and one instance below. We still use the route of the roads he drove across the Moor, and we can still see the farms he established. Some did well, or at any rate survived – Cornham, Horsen, Wintershead, Driver, Warren, Honeymead (owned by a family who number among its members a lord mayor of London). I have seen Driver; I have been past the signposts to Horsen and Wintershead; and I once got ticked off for camping on the land of Warren Farm without having asked for permission. One grew very big – Emmett's Grange – and that is the one I think was bought by Paul McCartney. If I am wrong, I shall no doubt soon be corrected.

However, it is the ones which did *not* survive that are the most evocative. I have seen two of them – Larkbarrow and Tom's Hill. Ruins now, of course. One can still see the line of trees planted on their northern edge, to weaken the force of the wind. They really are pretty bleak places. I should think you would have needed the grit and determination of the old Wild West sod-busters to make a go of it. Failure or not, ruin or not, there still lingers a palpable atmosphere. The Romans had a word – *numen* – to indicate a spirit, a presence that was not entirely of this world. Well, these were – are – numinous places.

That was, as I said, above ground. Below was copper. Quite a lot of it. The Knights planned to make a local industry out of the mining of it. Maybe even rival their counterpart in Cornwall. For a while, it looked like succeeding, but it didn't last. Cheaper, foreign minerals undercut the domestic product. Perhaps the Knights ran short of money, short of energy, short of interest, or short of energetic members of the family willing to work there; after all, reclaiming an ancient moor and extracting a mineral from below the earth are not cheap or easy activities. And there was the small matter of the great agricultural depression of the last quarter of the nineteenth century. So all that is left, we are told, is one shaft, one hole, at Wheal Eliza ('wheal' is a Cornish word for 'mine').

It was going to be only a matter of time before I became acquainted with the *Exmoor Review*, an annual publication put out by the Exmoor Society. It was not that I was converted to being any kind of precious devotee; it was simply that I was finding out two things: one, that there was a great deal of interest all around New Mill; and two, that there were many ways in which one could find out about it. And the *Exmoor Review* was one of them.

Take the issue for 1969. There was the usual variety of articles which one might expect from such a specialised kind of survey: history, archaeology, local interests like hunting and walking, wild life, Exmoor characters, and so on. As is often the case, it was the bits and pieces that attracted attention. The magazine received various new books which they were willing to review. One clearly indispensable piece of reading, which everyone should become familiar with, was *Brass Rubbing in Devon Churches*. Should be on everyone's bookshelf.

Scattered like pepper were spicy little anecdotes: 'Your wife is much younger than you, isn't she?' ' 'Er 'll get old quick enough.'

You would expect adverts from local businesses and service-providers, and you certainly got them. But it was a surprise to see a nation-wide organisation which thought it was worth putting in news about themselves. The Society of Authors, no less, announced its existence. Was it that the Exmoor area had authors – professional, amateur, and would-be – thicker on the ground than usual? Or did the S. of A. do this in every local interest magazine? If so, it would seem a pretty big regular chore.

Finally – always a winner – the personal adverts. Hotels and guest houses galore. Stamps for sale – 'British and New Zealand'. *New Zealand?* A ploughman's lunch at three shillings and sixpence. That is, 17½p. A three-course lunch in Dulverton for 37½p. Also for sale (this has to be true; I couldn't possibly have thought it up): 'FOR SALE – DIAPHRAGM PUMP, with two lengths pipe, foot-valve and strainer – all as new, cost over £20. Accept £10 or near offer. Box No. 1.'

Well, you think of a comment.

11

Expanding

It had never crossed my mind, when I first took on New Mill, that I would ever come to live there permanently, much less that I would come to live there with a wife and family. Which just goes to show you, doesn't it?

The 1950's radio comedian Al Read once put on a sketch in which the same question was put to a thousand different men. They were asked: 'Why did you get married?' According to the joke, over seventy per cent replied, 'I sometimes wonder.'

All right, it could imply regret, but it could also suggest a certain bewilderment at the speed and thoroughness with which the process was completed. Not only had I acquired a wife; I had acquired a couple of stepsons too, all fairly rapidly. There I was, at the beginning of 1971, with a house to organise, a new job to face, a new school to find for the two boys, and the means of transport to be seen to (you don't survive at New Mill in the late twentieth century with only a stout pair of shoes and a bicycle – and I didn't drive).

Why move then? Good question.

In a word – space. I had lived for eight years in a small bachelor flat, which was clearly going to be inadequate for the needs of three other people. New Mill may have been short of many things, but there was one thing it was not short of – space.

South-East England *was* (and is) – as one or two people may know – short of space. What space was available was cripplingly expensive. Well, it was for an assistant teacher with three more mouths to feed.

New Mill, looking back, was an answer. Maybe, in the opinion of many who may read this, not the best answer. But it was the obvious one. Enough bedrooms, a big lounge, a kitchen, a new bathroom and flush toilet (Ken had at last seen to that), an enormous garden, room to move, privacy, and your own river. True, you had to put into the equation weeds, nettles, brambles, cobbles, a steep and unmetalled lane, smoke, stone floors, a collapsing garage, a lopsided workshop, low lintels, peeling plaster, and sundry other engaging features which momentarily escape me.

But I have left the best till last. £2 a week. Even nearly fifty years ago that was impossibly cheap.

However, I have also left till last the biggest factor *missing* from the equation – a job.

Well, that was the prospect. Now that the equation had been spelt out (if indeed one does spell out equations), there remained the small matter of the decision. We spent the whole summer holiday at New Mill. Casing the joint, if you like. No matter how rosy the spectacles, no matter how romantic the idea of a cosy country cottage at the bottom of a hill beside a river, actually doing it was another matter. It was one thing to have New Mill as a holiday retreat, where one could live like a gypsy if so disposed, and be comforted by the thought that one could escape at any time back to the comfortable flat in the depths of civilisation. It was quite another to contemplate a permanent move of everything – with no prospect of escape, or even respite, when the going got tough.

However, there is one thing to be said for necessity: it saves a lot of debate. Given the situation I was in, and given the opportunity that New Mill represented, there did not seem to be much choice. It was no good saying that I should have been prudent and floated a mortgage several years before. I hadn't, and that was that. And the Home Counties was not exactly the ideal place to start down that road.

So we spent most of the summer holiday, by and large, getting used to the place as a family, and enjoying it. Frankly, I cannot remember lengthy and agonised discussions about the pros and cons. By the end of August, it seemed somehow taken for granted that we would give it a go.

All that remained was to come down to Devon again during the October half-term and look for a job for me. All!

Devon is a big place, but it does not have a big population. Towns tend to get spread out over a large area. Everything is a long way away. Take a look at the map. Once you have considered Barnstaple, Bideford, Ilfracombe, and, at a pinch, Tiverton, that is about it. If you want a job in a grammar school, that is. I had had one for over eleven years, and had been at home in it, so it was only natural that I should look for a means to continue that way of life. Anything further from New Mill would not have been practicable.

You have to be very optimistic indeed (or very driven by necessity) to expect to turn up in a grammar school straight off the street, and find a headmaster at that very moment racking his brains about where he is going to find a new teacher. But that, believe it or not, is what happened.

I had spoken to headmasters in Barnstaple, Ilfracombe, and Bideford (not distant Tiverton – I was not that desperate – well, not yet), and had drawn a blank each time. Worse, it was getting dangerously near the 31st of October, by which time protocol demanded that a teacher must submit his notice to his present headmaster, in order, naturally, to give that headmaster time to fill your post.

I had given it best, and was preparing to go back and face another term in my present school, and try again in the New Year. Right up against the wire, as you might say, our very last evening, the 31st of October, a neighbour came down the hill to give us a phone message. (New Mill, remember, did not boast a telephone.)

It seemed that the headmaster of Barnstaple Grammar School had just suffered the inconvenience which I have just described: one of his assistant teachers had handed in his notice on the very last day. He was right up against it. Would I care to come into Barnstaple to see him, with a view to starting work there in January?

Well, I had a look at my engagement diary, and found that I could indeed care to come into Barnstaple. My wife had been able to buy a Mini with the aid of a legacy, and we duly presented ourselves at his office.

I was a little taken aback to be told that the member of staff about to take off on his travels was not a History teacher, but an English one. Would I be able to take 'A' Level English? Yes, of course I could. (Thank God he didn't ask me what my experience was of 'A' Level English. Perhaps he didn't dare, in case I said 'None'.) There was a scattering of other mid-school classes, of course, both English and History. Could I do that? Yes, I thought I could. If he had said Politics and Economics, I should have said the same.

So that was the deal. I was just congratulating myself on my *coup*, and sparing an offhand vote of thanks to the Almighty, when he added a postscript.

'I have to tell you that this is for only two terms. It's a sort of permanent supply post. At the end of two terms, it will be advertised, and you can apply along with all the other applicants.' I could apply for my own job.

Good God! Now what? But before I said 'Yes', I did try one more question. I said to him, 'If someone made an offer like that to you, would you take it?'

He said, 'No.'

Few men in his difficult position would have said that. I warmed to him straight away.

I warmed to my current headmaster too. By the time I had got back to the flat and gone into work, it was past the 31st October deadline. Not far past it, but past. He would have been quite within his rights to refuse my request. Moreover, it was his first term in office, and he must have been concerned to get things right, cautious, circumspect, attentive to the rules. To his great credit, and my great relief, he said all right. So all I had to do was do it.

I had had one piece of encouragement. My mother and step-father had been in need of temporary accommodation (long story, and quite irrelevant), so I suggested New Mill. This was in the autumn, before I moved myself. They took up the idea, blind, as you might say. My mother had seen New Mill only once, in midwinter, and my stepfather not at all. They were well into pensioner age. They had no car.

They had a go. And they survived. And they soon had a fund of hilarious stories about the scrapes they had got into. So I thought, if they can do it. . .

The 17th of December was a date that became memorable – well, to me. I had been up to all hours the night before, helping the removal men. One particular chore sticks in the mind: we had to get a Collard and Collard upright piano down three flights of stairs to the van.

On the day itself, I had to complete my last-minute administration at my school, say goodbye to my colleagues, and to quite a lot of boys (I was a housemaster), pack a couple of stepsons into the back of a Mini, along with a Labrador pup we had acquired, clear the flat, drive over two hundred miles (well, I didn't of course; my wife did), and creep down New Mill Lane very late at night with two sleep-walking children (there was no way a Mini could get safely *down*, never mind up).

Mercifully we were greeted by my mother and stepfather, now seasoned veterans, who had made the necessary preparations. We had enough wit left to open our mouths when food was offered, and enough strength to clamber up the open-tread, bare wood stairs before falling into bed and into instant sleep.

We had started on our chosen course.

*

The hurdles came soon. Two will suffice by way of example. Christmas was the first, only eight days after the move. I had taken a drop in salary in order to take the Barnstaple job – the one that was going to last only two terms – so it was a somewhat 'austerity' festival. If that use of that word grates a little, may I remind you that this was 1970. The War had finished only twenty-five years before, and the vast majority of people easily remembered it. 'Austerity' had figured imperishably in their experience – food rationing, cheap versions, shortages, making do, economising. So, to our generation, the word 'austerity' came easily. We had a deep memory of it, and we still remembered how to cope with it.

For a tree I went out on to Ilkerton ridge and scavenged for a rotten, lichen-plastered branch of an appropriate size. It may not have pleased the Prince Consort (who I am given to understand introduced Christmas trees into England), and it certainly did not measure up to the perfect, scrumptious, tinsel-bedizened, Blackpool-illuminations masterpieces that you see in Hollywood films. But it was green, and knobbly, and gnarled, and twisted, and generally a mite exotic, so it fitted the mood of the season. We could choose any size we wanted. It was right on our doorstep. It did not shed needles all over the place. It did not have to be ensconced in a pot. There were lots of angles and twists and jagged joints to hang things from. And it was free. One could do a lot worse.

Food purchases were careful, but nobody went hungry. Drink was a little more rationed – none of your Lucullan range of spirit bottles on the sideboard, or trays of lager in the fridge. I think we had some wine, and maybe stretched to a bottle of sherry. Indeed, it was nearly twenty years before a bottle of wine with dinner became a regular Sunday fixture, and I say that not as a champion of temperance or as a dyed-in-the-wool Pharisee but as the guardian of the public purse. The drink rate was governed not by morals or self-righteousness but by the exchequer.

We managed a fair selection of presents for the boys, but there was no question of Christmas-pattern wrapping paper, coloured sellotape, and ducky little labels attached with glistening string. I sat on the floor with each present between my legs, and enveloped them in acres of newspaper. At least they would have the fun of an involved unwrapping process. If you think about it, the unwrapping is half the fun. So they got plenty of that.

No problem with a fire, of course. None of your impersonal radiators, storage heaters, fans, and stoves. None of your blocked-in, hygienic, ever-so-convenient flameless hearths. We had the real thing – logs and ashes and fireguards and woodsmoke (you soon got used to a generous ration of that; no austerity there).

No television – imagine, a Christmas without Arthur Askey and Billy Smart's Circus, *The Sound of Music*, and Christmas night party with the stars. How did we survive the deprivation?

So – on the whole, by and large, and taking things all round – we didn't do too badly. I have noticed, many times, how often, and how quickly, the family can fall to reminiscing about New Mill generally. Maybe some of the stories get a mite taller with the years, but something must have started them off. New Mill, it seems, had, and has, the trick of memorability.

I think the same thing applied to the boys' new school, Lynton County Primary. At whatever age one may be, very few clap hands at the jolly prospect of a new school. So it is to Christopher's and Martin's credit that they got the measure of Lynton as soon, and as well, as they did.

The headmaster, to begin with, was a trifle – shall we say? – unusual. Harold Jester was a law unto himself. One of Nature's eccentrics. Tall, rangy, not the nattiest of dressers. Soft-voiced. You would have expected a headmaster to have a sort of sergeant-major timbre to his vocal chords. Not this one. But you would also guess that the children under his authority would have minded their behaviour, for fear of what he might notice. For Harold was astigmatic; his eyes did not focus properly, so you never knew the direction in which he was looking. He was well aware of the effect he had; he regularly made jokes about it.

This can be disconcerting for adults too. I don't know about you, but, on the admittedly rare occasions on which I find myself talking to someone with this trouble, I unfailingly find myself looking at the wrong eye. I would suddenly come to with a jolt, because I would notice the real eye looking at me very directly, and almost saying, 'I am over here.' You almost want to apologise for prying.

In cases where the wandering eye did not achieve the level of order he considered consonant with sound education, Harold would have no compunction about falling back on the slipper. Again, one must remember that in 1970, the 'developed' world was not paranoid as it is today, about possible harmful effects on children of a huge range of activities and practices which they had been cheerfully surviving for decades. Nowadays, not only is corporal punishment frowned upon – indeed regarded with horror; the same righteous wrath is being directed at selection, streaming, grammar schools, rugby football, competitive sports, single-sex schools, cross-country running, Latin and Greek, and brightly-coloured mineral waters.

It was not totally accepted even in Harold's time, but he ran his school as he wished, and, so far as I know, he suffered no more than an average ration of complaint, interference, and bossiness from parents. By the same token, he answered correspondence when he felt like it; he never allowed himself to be disturbed by inspectors, advisers, parents' associations, and red tape generally. I wonder what he would have done with emails today.

For all that, I received the impression that Lynton Primary was a pretty contented place. Harold must have kept them busy – always an infallible recipe for good order. For instance, on the famed annual excursions to London, the day would be interminable. London was a long way away. At a beat-the-milkman hour of the morning, buses to Barnstaple and trains to Paddington; or coaches all the way. And then a frantic tour of exhibitions, shows, towers of London, museums, and 'sights' in general. By the time they came home, they were on their knees.

Harold also had a pretty good idea of the abilities and potential of his pupils. For example, he saw to it that Christopher sat with a boy called Edmund. Both were bright, and both believed that school was a place where you worked and had a chance to prove yourself. Not for them the rough and tumble and two fingers to authority of farm lads and apple-scrumpers.

Harold had accurately pegged both of them. They may well have gravitated together without Harold's initiative, I don't know, but gravitate they did. They stayed friends right through the separation of secondary school (they went to different ones) and university (different ones again), and they are friends to this day.

Martin, the younger one, was a different prospect.

Rather like Harold Jester, Martin made his own way. He behaved himself, he paid attention, he listened to what the teacher was telling him, and then he carried on with what he had been doing in the first place. We were not worried about this, because it was a reflection of what we knew of him at home.

What did worry us was the fact that he did not seem to be making the progress that one would have expected from a six- or seven-year-old. He never pushed himself forward. Whether it was due to shyness or lack of confidence we did not yet know. My guess was that lack of confidence was not the problem; otherwise he would not have been so politely obstinate in class, when given all that advice, and then going his own way. There was some factor we had not yet tumbled to.

He did not speak clearly. This was no doubt owing to a tongue-tie that he was born with. Apparently his tongue did not have the mobility of average tongues. Well, he couldn't help that, poor lad.

Most worrying of all was his level of reading. Even at eight or nine, he could not be said to have mastered it. Sums, yes. Reading, no.

It was Christopher who was seen as the successful one, the one with a fine future before him. He was used to success, and he was used to praise. Martin just bowled along quite unconcerned, either by his lack of formal 'success' or by our disquiet over it. But it was interesting to note that, when a mathematical problem came up to face both of them, it was Christopher who was struggling with the rules, and it was Martin who had worked it out almost by instinct. This baffled Christopher; it just didn't seem right. Martin, again, went his way.

Harold had spotted all this. Whenever we met him and expressed our concern about Martin's apparent lack of progress, he would say, 'You don't have to worry about Martin; he has all his marbles and he has them in the right order. He will do fine.'

Like all good schoolmasters, he had read his pupil correctly, as he had read Christopher. It wasn't the tongue-tie. It wasn't the recent change of schools. It wasn't the fact that he had moved from a well-breeched suburban primary to a slow-moving rural one. It wasn't the fact that he was rebelling against a recently-acquired step-father. (Well, I suppose he might have been, but I don't think it would have come out in a tongue-tie or an inability to read. It would have come out in some other way.)

He simply wasn't moving forward on all fronts, as Christopher seemed to be.

But, in the long run, Harold was completely vindicated. The only person in the immediate family with a First-Class Honours degree is Martin. And he did it in Maths. As a footnote, years later, one of his sons got a First – in Philosophy.

Exmoor winter gate

12

Meeting More

Coming to live somewhere, after having paid it only the attention of an infrequent holiday trip, presents a different prospect. True, I was still a foreigner from 'up Lunnon way' – or a 'grockle', if you like. So that hadn't changed. There was no way I could suddenly convince them that I had become a Devonian. I had no greater hope of success by the simple fact of dwelling there. I had not suddenly acquired a whole battery of skills which would enable me to tackle New Mill with a greater hope of taming it; so I was still going to need help. It was going to be a little more than Stan Marsh leaving me a box of groceries by the railway bridge every time my holidays began. That hadn't changed either.

Nor was I the only stranger in the family; my wife was from Kingston, and the two boys had been born in the Home Counties as well. All three had 'south-east' written all over them. And that didn't fade. You might expect that children of six and eight, with minds and memories like blotting paper, would have absorbed something of Devon speech and culture, rubbing shoulders as they did with Lynton kids in the playground. Later, too, when they went to comprehensive schools in Ilfracombe and Barnstaple. Not a bit of it. And when Stephen was born, he too remained south-east. However, he did show that he had an ear; he could appreciate the local accent, and he could put it on when so moved. But the other two couldn't even do that. They took on a lot of Devon, and it has remained firmly in their memory, and their imagination (and, I hope, their affections). Witness the way the stories get taller every year. But, when we moved from New Mill and went to Barnstaple, and when they both finally left home – Christopher to university and Martin to the RAF – they both sounded as totally 'south-east' as they had done when they arrived.

In a word – well, three actually – we were different. I have often wondered what our neighbours must have thought of us – most unlikely colonists to say the least. Nor did we show (at first; I hope it got better as time passed) much sign of making the grade. Country-dwellers have seen more than their fair share of townees who have embarked on their Great Adventure of 'living in the country', of 'getting away from it all' (whatever 'it' is), of 'getting out of the rat race' (whatever *that* is). For all I know they may have made a wry face and given us six months.

I think what may have made us different was the fact that this was no 'adventure'. Circumstances had worked out in such a way that we didn't have much choice. I won't say it was New Mill or nothing, but it was probably New Mill or not much. And at least it was, like us, different.

We were not left to muddle through. Well, we did muddle through, but we were not alone in our muddling. For example, David Leworthy helped us with getting the piano down New Mill Lane. Ken Beauchamp, when he was there, mended things and fixed things and shored things up (much of it with pink binder twine of course), and serviced the pump in Mole's Chamber. John Leworthy made his telephone available when we needed to make, or receive, important calls. The family running the stables and guest house up the valley had two sons who soon added their company to the boys' rural education. Miss Blackmore, naturally, adopted us.

*

Leaving aside for the moment that we all had to live, eat, drink, sleep, go to work or school, and generally survive, what else did we do?

I learnt to drive for a start. Well, it was both obvious and necessary. I learnt in Mrs. Coates' Mini. I had had some lessons from a fellow-subaltern during National Service in Kenya, but the memory of them had almost completely faded. The only clear recollection that remained was of the time when Ray (Ray Bernard – his family lived in Kenya, and, before that, in Java) introduced me to clutch control. Having shown me the principle of it, he said, 'Now do it; edge forward slowly.' Slowly! To make his point, he stood facing me, about eight feet in front of my bumper. He held up both hands and made come-hither movements with his fingers.

I was horrified. I knew all about learners' rabbit leaps. Indeed I already had a few vintage ones to my own credit. But to edge towards his knees only eight, seven, six feet away. And it was an old Chevrolet. A very old Chevrolet.

'Come on, come on. Don't worry about me; just concentrate.' I did. The man famously said that you can't beat a firing squad for concentrating the mind. Well, I can tell you that a learner's experience of edging a venerable Chevrolet towards someone's knees only feet away came a very respectable second. I nearly slipped only once, but Ray had some kind of instinct which enabled him to skip to one side. I have always admired his nerve. I think he had more judgment than the average, and more understanding of the assessment of risk, and that may have been because, as a boy, he had survived three years in a Japanese internment camp during the War. More simply, he had a cooler head. He was certainly no ordinary young man.

Anyway, I got a whiff of that memory as I sat in the driving seat of the Mini for the first time. Mini bonnets are anything but prodigious, but this one seemed to stretch for infinity. I could snatch no impression of how outside objects related to it. I simply didn't know where anything was. For a split second I was prey to one of the most desolate feelings of helplessness I can remember. This monster was going to be ungovernable. That bonnet stretched before me as if it belonged to Cruella de Vil's Rolls.

But of course I learnt, and I am smugly proud to announce that I passed first time.

That ushered in another problem, as every solution always does.

Who was going to drive the Mini? Since my wife has always regarded a day behind the wheel as a day well spent, and since fourteen per cent of her bloodstream is pure petrol, I had to look for another vehicle. There was one other reason too: it was her Mini, the fruit of a legacy from a beloved aunt.

I forget now the mechanics of the search, but I came up with a second-hand Land Rover. A very second-hand Land Rover (fourth or fifth-hand, I should think, if the truth be told). To give you some idea of its age, its number plate read 'UYB 34'.

When features like cruise control, anti-skid brakes, air conditioning, satnavs, heated seats, dashboards like theatre organs, and I don't know what, have become standard, it may take an effort of the imagination to picture what I had bought (admittedly for not very much). It was little more than a tin box to look at. When you shut the doors, it sounded like one too. It had the famous Land-Rover innards of course, with its famous high- and low-gear ratios, but my guess is that the mileometer had gone right round the clock two or three times. Bits of material and other equipment drooped off the inside walls. There were burst cushions on the metal seats. Apart from that, nothing. There were more bare nuts and bolts, edges, cracks, and corners than you would find underneath a steam locomotive – near-death traps for the unwary or the unlucky.

The longevity of the engine had given it a raucous roar evocative of Louis Armstrong with laryngitis. There was no danger of my knocking anyone over, unless they were stone deaf; you could hear me coming for miles. So that was something, I suppose.

But it got me to work, in the very worst weathers too – all those low gears. However, there was one dark February evening when the windscreen wipers packed up, just when I was trying to get home through the snow for Stephen's (my new son) first birthday. I didn't make it; the poor lad was on his way to bed when I finally arrived. No mobiles to tell them I was going to be late. Even if I had had one, I couldn't ring them up; we were not on the phone. And even if we had had a mobile at home, down in that valley there was next to no signal.

The maintenance of this antique soon began to be very costly. Luckily I had made the acquaintance of a very willing and hard-working mechanic at Blackmoor Gate, about half-way between New Mill and Barnstaple, and he shored up clutches and gear-boxes and things. One of his favourite methods of dealing with lesser complaints was to feel around the stricken area, fish a claw-head hammer out of his tool-box, and administer a wince-making whack to some harmless body work that was minding its own business. When I passed comment on this, to me, rather random technique, he grinned and said, 'Ah, but you have to know *where* to whack it – and how hard.'

However, this could not go on. The doors, as I said, were loose and rattly, and, frankly, little more substantial than sardine cans. One evening I was in Barbrook, and had occasion to do a U-turn (it's all right; there was no traffic, and the road was wide at that point). As I swung round, the passenger door, never very secure, came adrift, swung right out – and came off.

It may be a common occurrence for a driver to have to leap out and rescue a wayward spanner or a scarf that he had forgotten about on the roof; but I don't think many of us have had the mortification of climbing out of the driving seat and collecting a door from the roadway, glancing anxiously to left and right in the hope that nobody was looking.

It says something once again the for vehicle's primitiveness that I was able to pick the whole unit up and re-attach it with no trouble at all – as if it were a piece of Meccano. But I drove home very carefully.

The event must have set in motion a subconscious train of thought. One day, shortly afterwards, as I was driving home, and pondering the latest garage bill that had dropped on our mat courtesy of Joe Pyall, our patient postman, I had one of those rare epiphanies which historians and story-tellers have attributed to famous men. You know – Sir Isaac looking up into the tree and wondering whether the impact of the apple was based on science or on a particularly malevolent and capricious Cox's orange pippin.

Or Charles Darwin looking at all those specimens spread across his desk and speculating as to whether they all had something to do with each other.

Well, mine was just as dramatic, though I can not claim that it dictated the future direction of science. But it was momentous for me. A thunderbolt of insight descended as I negotiated the hairpin bends near Shirwell. I suddenly thought, 'If I can afford to pay all these bills for an old Land-Rover, I can afford the hire-purchase payments for a new one.' I bet not many people are blessed with inspirations and insights like that.

There was the small matter of borrowing the money for the deposit. My mother and stepfather did the honours for that, and away I went to the County Garage in Barnstaple, where, after an appropriate wait for delivery, I negotiated the princely price of £1,500 for a brand-new, shiny, sparkling (and much quieter) Land Rover. Fifteen hundred pounds!

It became known, of course, as the 'new' Land Rover, for years. Fifteen in fact. When I finally sold it, we were still thinking of it as the 'new' Land Rover.

I have been lucky with Land Rovers – well, lucky for a man who has no instinct for bargaining, and knows next to nothing about the second-hand car market. For a variety of reasons which now escape me, I sold the old one for more than I paid for it – well, just. I later heard that it was still doing duty hauling boats and things across the shingle on a distant Devon beach.

I did even better with the new one. Remember, I had paid £1,500 for it. Well, when, fifteen years later, a prospective buyer turned up and gave it a trial run, and asked me what I had in mind for the price, I took a deep breath, and, bearing in mind the effect of 15 years of inflation, and having had just sufficient wit to glance beforehand at a couple of motoring magazines, wondered out loud if he could be prepared to meet an asking price of £2,000. To my amazement, he replied, 'Mr. Coates, I wouldn't dream of offering you any less.' So there. Maybe it proves my point about being no good at bargaining; perhaps I should have asked a lot more.

*

We came to know a lot more people, not just as casual faces that popped up every two or three months during holidays, but people you actually lived with in the community.

Take food. We could not continue to rely on the occasional cardboard box from Stan Marsh at Caffyn's. That meant the International at Lynton. Yes, they had got as far as supermarkets in 1971. It wasn't very big; you could get it into a modern Sainsbury's about fifty times over. But it served.

If you wanted more personal attention, you could walk eighty yards up the main road and go to Rumbelow's. There you could rely on being served by the owners. Either Pop Rumbelow, or Ron, his son. I believe the counters were dark brown wood. They weren't so primitive as to have sawdust on the floor, and I can't remember whether or not a bell rang when you went in. But I do have a recollection of pyramids of tins, wooden boxes, and bacon-slicing machines. And there was Ron, leaning expectantly forward, with hands spread on the counter before him, hanging on your every word, ready to leap to find, locate, detect, search for, dig out, stretch towards anything you wanted. His memory of course was encyclopaedic. He could have found anything he wanted blindfold.

I don't know if he and his Dad had a greater range of stock, and I can not at this distance of time recall whether his prices were higher or lower than the International's. But that wasn't the point. The point was the personal element. You were getting individual attention; your every request was seen to; you were actually being served. I know that most supermarket staff these days are knowledgeable, helpful, and polite, but it's not the same. It's the difference between worshipping in a cathedral and praying in your own village church. Shopping with Ron Rumbelow was so therapeutic.

It was the same with Richards' ironmongery, along by the fish and chip shop. The same set-up too. Old Man Richards ran the place with his son. Keith. If you thought it was a feat of memory to find anything in Rumbelow's, you should have seen the variety of stock in Richards. At least you could classify pretty well everything Ron sold as 'food', but no such elementary portmanteau word would have sufficed for the Aladdin's cave of Richards: carpenter's supplies, pots, kindling, string, garden tools, paint, oil, domestic gadgets, the list stretched out. Supplies littered the counter, stock was piled up in corners, bags and sacks almost blocked aisles, miscellanea hung from the ceiling, bulged from groaning shelves, and tripped up the unwary. Frying pans, paraffin lamps and heaters, household electric equipment, broom handles, fusewire, garden twine – it went on. If it were not for the fact you had to eat, you could sustain domestic life by shopping at Richards. I don't think they sold clothes as such, but I bet you could have bought oilskins, dungarees, overalls, protective gloves, and Wellington boots there.

As with the Rumbelows, Richards, father and son, knew everything, and remembered where everything was. They were a fount of advice, old-fashioned wisdom, and recipes and suggestions for dealing with practically every domestic crisis that a malignant fate could inflict.

Come out of Richards, having refilled your five-gallon paraffin drum, turn right, walk past the dairy and the laundry (a real laundry, not a launderette), past the alley that led to the workshop of Harry Horrabin (billed to the tourists as the oldest working blacksmith in England), past a pub and a hotel, and there, facing you, was a family butcher, with a name that, if I had not seen it over the shop with my own eyes, I would not have believed.

Fouracre. I assure you – Fouracre. If you had been writing a saga of country life a couple of generations ago, and had named one of your characters 'Fouracre', no editor would have worn it. And – *and* – that wasn't the end of it. His Christian name was Fred. Freddy Fouracre. Imagine.

He was one of the most cheery men you could wish to meet. He always had a smile on his face, which was usually of a jolly, Father-Christmas reddish hue. Like Ron Rumbelow, he at once gave you his full attention. He would lean forward, rub his hands, and say, 'What would you like then?' Because he had said it so many times, he had achieved a mastery of elision that no punctuation or spelling could do justice to. It came out as something like 'whashulikethen?' He got the 'like' and the 'then', but that was all.

He had a wife called Freda, we discovered, though, like Captain Mainwaring's wife Elizabeth, she never actually appeared – well, not in the shop. The money was taken and change doled out by a lady encased in a glass cabinet at the back. You never saw her enter or leave this cage. The only thing that moved was her hands, though she was known to smile from time to time. It could be that, like Lenin, she had been embalmed, and only the upper half of her body had survived the ravages of decomposition. And, believe it or not, her name was Freda too.

*

Because of the boys, we became familiar with the primary school, where Harold Jester reigned in eccentric but discerning pomp. His wife worked there too, and divided her attention between her class and five of their own children. Harold, I suspect, must have been something of a handful, because she had a slightly distant, tooth-sucking, long-suffering air, which however could be relieved by the occasional dry, deadpan observation. But you could never imagine anybody imposing on Barbara; she was very much her own woman.

She had the trick of making you notice her without making any effort to create an impression. She was, in many ways, the opposite of the lady who dealt with the very young ones. Melanie Hornby was one of Nature's irresistible forces. She was like the tide coming in.

That verdict represents not criticism but benign admiration. She was definite, forceful, articulate, and entertaining. For all her apparent dragon-like qualities, her pupils were very happy with her. I'm sure they were never tempted to take liberties, but she was so sure and confident that they felt secure; so long as 'Miss Hornby' was around, there was nothing much that could go wrong.

Small children away from parents could at times feel very *in*secure. Melanie had her own way of dealing with that: she had on hand a large cardboard box; whenever one of her infants felt that the world was a little too much, she put them in the box – safe, quiet, private. I shouldn't think any text-book on infant psychology would have had a reference to anything like that, but for Melanie it was a classic case of common sense. Genius in its simplicity.

This was the key to so much of Melanie's approach. She was your genuine eccentric; everyone else thought her behaviour was extraordinary, even perhaps outrageous, but to her it was the most blinding common sense.

In case this makes her appear like some loud, ego-driven boa-constrictor, I must add that she was unfailingly concerned for the welfare of her children, and felt genuine outrage if any of them was unfairly treated.

One day she told us about one of her boys who had been invited to a birthday party in the town – or *thought* he had been invited to a birthday party. He duly turned up at the front door, clutching a birthday present for the lucky one. The mother opened the door, looked down at him, and said, 'There must be some mistake; we didn't invite you.' Not content with that, she relieved him of the present, and shut the door in his face.

Melanie was incandescent at the injustice, and at the pain the boy must have suffered.

On other occasions, she could enliven any gathering, simply by talking about ordinary things which had happened to her. Only with Melanie they were not ordinary; they were hilarious. All right, so she liked to be the queen bee; you always knew when Melanie was in the room; nobody else mattered. But it was done not by loudness, or bad manners, or conceit, or 'pushiness'; it was done by sheer force of personality. She couldn't help it.

There was a celebrity clergyman at the turn of the eighteenth and nineteenth centuries called the Revd. Sydney Smith. He was not blue-blooded; he was not well-connected; and he was not rich. He lived in small village rectory in Somerset most of the time. However, he had a reputation, and a well-deserved reputation, for being the funniest man in London. So, whenever he was able to escape from Somerset (he described living in the country as 'a healthy grave'), he became a regular feature of the social season, because hosts, and especially hostesses, vied with each other to have such an entertaining man on their guest list.

Many stories were told of guests practically falling off their chairs in helpless laughter as they listened to him, but nobody afterwards could give a totally satisfactory explanation of exactly what he had said that was so funny. People tried, but the task eluded them. One very sceptical lady of mature years voiced her opinion that his reputation was over-stated. Nobody, she said, could be that funny. She was invited to attend one of his 'evenings' herself. It is said that, long before the end of the meal, she had to be assisted from the table.

Well, Melanie was like that. She was not necessarily funny – although at times she could be very funny indeed. It was simply that she was always worth listening to – much more so than anybody else in the room. But to relate what she actually said would give no impression of her impact.

I daresay there were plenty of people who found her hard to take – mostly women, I suspect. But you could never doubt her sincerity or her integrity. And I for one always felt better for having spent some time in her company.

We came to see more of her than one might expect because, after two or three years, Mrs. Coates secured the job of school secretary. It is a position of great authority and influence. Ask any pupil or any headmaster. School secretaries, especially primary school secretaries, are like popes; their power is absolute and it is eternal. Headmasters come and go; school secretaries go on for ever.

We used to go to parents' evenings, naturally, but because of Mrs. Coates' position (I nearly said 'status') we also attended other social gatherings held at the school. The one that sticks most clearly in the mind was a sort of indoor fête. At least, it turned out to be more of an indoor occasion because for most of that Saturday afternoon it rained cats and dogs.

One of the attractions was a competition for pets. A dog show. I can't think how or why we allowed ourselves to be talked into it, but we arrived with our canine member, to be offered as a candidate. Now dear old Snowball was of a certain age, and very, very domestic. None of the primping and preening for her. You could have groomed her for a week, and she would have looked just the same. We knew nothing of her pedigree. She looked like a West Highland terrier, but we had no means of knowing whether a mongrel with a roving eye had ever had an assignation with her great-grandmother. She ambled through life entirely on her own terms, and was impressed by nothing. Awe and fear did not enter her vocabulary. If an elephant had broken into the house, Snowball would have taken it on without a moment of hesitation.

She was certainly not fazed by a primary school dog show. She didn't care what she looked like when up against all these statuesque, well-combed creatures that strutted and fretted their hour on the classroom stage.

She won a prize. They must have been a bit stuck to describe her classification. She was deemed the best entry in 'Dogs Various'.

13

Burning and Warming

Which would you rather be – too hot or too cold? Let us hope that a capricious deity never presents us with such a dire choice in life. But I fancy that I could produce an answer to the riddle. Easy of course when the question is only an academic exercise, but I can, I think, produce some evidence to shore up the logic of my answer.

When I was a student, I lived for two years on the top floor of a huge, seventeenth-century stone building. Come to think of it, not far from the age of New Mill. I had two rooms there, a sitting room and a bedroom. Wasn't I lucky, visitors would say, to have so much space, and to be in such impressive, imposing, 'traditional' accommodation.

Well, yes. But I spent most of my time being grateful for having got into a university at all. I was not sophisticated or detached enough to have any views on the merits and defects of the architecture; I'd have been pleased to be anywhere.

However, as the months went by, I did come to form some opinions, not so much about my present accommodation as about whatever accommodation I should have in the future.

Summers, of course, were fine. Plenty of light up there, glorious views, a balcony on which one could sprawl on the back legs of one's chair and pretend to be revising for an exam. And warm.

Winters were different. No central heating, of course. No stoves. No fireplaces – well, none that still worked (they had presumably gone defunct round about the time of the Crimean War). The only heating came from a tiny gas fire in the sitting room. And you didn't turn that on very much because you were afraid of eating up your college grant. (Mine was £76 a term. Not just for gas; for food, rent, books, clothes, entertainment, everything.) If you sat close enough to feel the warmth, the fumes sent you to sleep; if you stayed far enough away to keep awake, you hardly felt any heat.

The bedroom was worse – no heating at all. And bare lino. Oh, and one small mat beside the bed. I once dropped a splash of water on the lino; it froze on impact. When I went to bed, sometimes, I would be wearing vest and pants under pyjamas, and socks. On the bed I piled every item of top clothing I could collect. In one particularly cold snap, I even put the mat on top of the bedclothes.

That experience did give me some views on domestic arrangements. However, they did not take the form of savage criticism of my surroundings; as I said, I was too grateful, almost incredulous, to be at university at all. So I could never have made any kind of complaint or organised a campaign of agitation. I was far too much in awe of the authorities.

No – my views took the shape of formulating policy for the future – assuming I survived the Siberian conditions of the present. It was not a conscious resolution, much less a vow. But I do remember saying to myself, in however vague a way, that, in my coming life, whatever other efforts I was to make towards my welfare and advancement, I was going to try and make sure that I was warm.

New Mill had a lot in common with my college rooms. Of a similar age, as I said. Possibly even older. It was made of stone. Solid, yes. But it made you pay for its solidity with its chill. Stone is cold. It was spacious – so, a lot of air to warm up. It had no central heating. The plaster on the walls left a lot to be desired. Carpets were in very short supply. And New Mill didn't even have a miniscule gas fire.

What with that, and what with my views on keeping the blood circulating, the top priority was pretty obvious.

Another similarity of course was that people thought it was

wonderful – 'traditional', 'idyllic', 'quintessentially English', and so on. But they didn't have to live there.

However, I had *chosen* to live there, so it was up to me to get on with it. I had to make my own heat, as it were. That meant fires and paraffin heaters.

Paraffin heaters, in actual fact, are not so primitive or crude or medieval as one who has never used them might think. *Passé*, maybe, but not inefficient. They have a lot going for them. They are relatively cheap to buy. Well they were when I bought mine. I have not checked up on Amazon recently. They are light and easy to carry around. On a low flame they can burn all day. All night too, if you don't mind filling them up twice every twenty-four hours instead of once. They are uncomplicated, and easy to maintain. When I say that they did not present an insuperable barrier to someone even of my Neanderthal mechanical skills, I hope I make my point.

Best of all, they gave out a delightful type of heat. No roaring flames, naturally. It sounds silly to say that they produced a comforting warm sort of heat, but that was in effect what they did. It was embracing; it filled the air, all over – no scorching burn close to and chill prospect far away. It was a gentle, comforting heat. When you entered a room (assuming it was not the Albert Hall), you knew at once that it was there, and it was pleasing. Dammit, it almost welcomed you.

So we had four paraffin heaters.

We also had a fireplace. So circumstances, the need for further comfort, and common sense dictated that we put a fire in it. Quaint old black beams and giant mantelpieces and dangling horse brasses were lovely, but they didn't provide heat.

I had met this problem of course when I first rented New Mill, way back in the prehistoric past before marriage. Ken, to his credit, gave freely of his time and ingenuity in a joint effort to make it efficient. We were up against lack of tools and facilities, and above all lack of knowledge. It was all very well to become familiar with grate construction and draught and chimney size and air currents and cowls and types of log and I don't know what. None of those made the fire go. It was like knowing how a carburettor worked and being familiar with clutches and spark plugs, and not being able to drive the thing.

Our chief bugbear, naturally, was smoke. Whatever we did about the arrangement of the fireplace, the height of the grate irons off the stone floor, and the agonising slowness with which the fire 'took', sooner or later smoke would billow out from the gaping hole of the hearth and we would be back to square one. One remark summed up our many efforts, our joint ignorance, and, to our credit, our cheerfulness in the face of constant frustration. It also gave away the fact that Ken had attended public school; a habit of speech from his youth surfaced as we sat low in chairs with our legs stretched out, either side of the fog factory, and contemplated our umpteenth failure.

'Harry smokers,' he said.

It was always a chancy business. You won some; you lost some. It was like the little girl with the curl on her forehead. When it was good, it was very, very good, and you basked in the glow and thought how boring and unromantic it was for all those benighted souls who lounged and yawned in front of electric bars or storage heaters. But when it was bad, you hoped that none of those benighted souls would put his head round the door and revel in your discomfiture.

Then, one day, I had a breakthrough. I was being driven particularly bananas by the thing. I had got it going, it had 'taken', some heat was permeating the room, and I thought it safe to go to the kitchen and prepare a meal. Surely, now it would behave itself once it knew who was boss.

Ten minutes later I came back, straight into the familiar smog and smut. I was furious. That was it. That was enough. I went straight outside, procured a bucket, held it under the waterfall, and returned to the lounge loaded for bear. It had done this once too often. Right!

And it got the lot right in the midriff. There was a lot of protest. Serve it right. I turned away in smug satisfaction and went to put the bucket back outside. When I came back, it was blazing both brightly and steadily, with not a wisp of smoke in sight. And it went on like that for the rest of the day.

I can not claim that I had got it tame, like Alexander breaking Bucephalus, but we achieved a sort of unpredictable mutual tolerance, the fire and I, a *modus vivendi*, as you might say. Well, you would if you had received the debatable benefits of several years of Latin instruction. A Latin education does not make you show off; it simply provides you with a greater choice of words and phrases to convey precision of expression. It gives you more shots in the linguistic locker.

This wary partnership concept characterised pretty well everything about New Mill. You never felt that you had won. Or, when you did, it would kick back, just to remind you that the contest wasn't over. Gas cylinders were fine, but, one hour of negligence or forgetfulness, and you could be suddenly faced with an empty one, and of course, it always happened in the evening, and you had to go and change over to a new one in the pouring rain outside – in the dark. Paraffin heaters could play you up too. You had to be the possessor of a near-infallible memory to keep track of everything. We had four, remember?

Remember too that the Land Rover also had a will of its own. It loved buggering up gear boxes, and breaking clutches and springing punctures. If all else failed, it could always make the windscreen wipers conk out or chuck one of the doors into the road.

Power cuts were not unknown. Hoses could come adrift and taps refuse to turn off completely when you were not looking. Mole's Chamber could seize up with congealed grease because you had forgotten to unclog it in your unceasing struggle with the Japanese knotweed. Second-hand mowers broke down. Fridges would ice up. (None of your self-defrosting miracles.) Behind it all, lurking like some kind of hibernating dragon, was the river, the water. You knew what it could do, and you knew that, if it did, there wasn't much alternative to an undignified evacuation. It was rather like the War: you could have a bomb drop on you every day for six years; you just didn't think about it. Perhaps, having survived the War, I was better equipped to deal with such a situation.

I suppose it gave you respect for the place. And there is nothing wrong with having respect for the house you live in. Keeps you on your toes.

I suppose, looking back, yes, I could have taken the whole place by the scruff of the neck – built roads, moved walls, raised ceilings, installed oil-fired central heating. But there were two things militating against it: one, it belonged to Ken, not me, and I was paying a minimal rent; and two, there was the inconvenient fact that I did not have enough income or capital to do much more than buy some pots of paint, never mind gut the place and rebuild it.

So you just did the next thing, and you continued the regular battle with the fire. One thing: it never got boring. There was always something happening.

Take the chimney fire. I can't remember how it started; for once I must have been more successful than usual in my pre-natal gropings in the grate. It just shows you how human the damn thing was. I had shown it who was boss, and drilled it into obedience sufficiently to produce a lovely blaze. So it kicked back. Before I knew where I was, the chimney was indeed on fire.

We had no hose. Only a ladder. I had to wiggle it out of the workshop, take it outside to the other end of the house, where the mill mechanism had once been, lean it against the wall immediately below the chimney, and climb up to make sure. The ladder would not reach the top of the chimney, but I saw enough to realise that yes, there was a fire all right, big enough to need putting out. Now what?

The only structure of the house that came close was the ruinous beam that ran from the wall of the chimney to the very last wall of the house – the ridge beam of a roof that was no longer there.

What did Superman do? He saw that the ladder was long enough to enable him to climb up and work himself, with considerable wobbling and indignity, into a position of a straddle across the beam. Then, clutching a full bucket, I edged and jolted my way along the beam, hoping fervently that no stray splinters would catch me through the trousers that masked my manhood. (Just imagine – eighteen or twenty feet off the ground, astride a centuries-old paint-stripped beam, jolting along inch by inch with a bucket of water in your hand, and you get a splinter in your – well, just imagine.). When I reached the other end, I was high enough – just – to be able to stretch up my arms, balance the bucket on the edge of the chimney, and tip the contents down the hole. I had to do this two or three times.

What I have described, or perhaps the way I describe it, may give the impression that I was behaving like some kind of Douglas Fairbanks (or, as I said, Superman), with not a nerve or a tremor in sight. In fact, it was one bloody great big shuffle and bumble. One thing was in my favour: I was so taken up with concentrating on my clever idea (no sensible handyman would have dreamed of tackling the job in anything like the way I did) that I do not remember being frightened. The task had required total focus.

It was only when I came down, looked up at the height of the chimney, the height of the beam, the ricketiness of it, and its age, that it began to dawn on me that what I had embarked upon was a mite dangerous. I felt scared then all right. No wonder Mrs. Coates said she had been rather nervous.

But I did put the fire out.

So – yes – looking back, it was a bit of a crisis. The other fire I was involved in was a completely different matter. We had no idea that there was any crisis at all.

When I say 'we', I mean Ken and myself. So this dates it to before New Mill became a family home.

As I hope I have made clear, running New Mill involved a great deal of cutting, hacking, sawing, dragging, clearing – and of piling up great pyres of it for burning. None of your smoke-free areas or self-righteous, nimby-pimby neighbours on the edge of Exmoor.

It was a favourite job for a long summer evening. The real hard work had been done – well, as much as we wanted to do; even Ken had to stop some time. Lighting a bonfire was a pleasant postscript to the day's labour. Bonfires are enjoyable things: they are good to watch; they are proof of how hard you have been working; the smell of earth and smoke is not unpleasant; you didn't even mind the smudge and smuts. You were covered in dried sweat from the other work anyway.

So Ken and I were there, one warm near-twilight, just standing around and gazing, occasionally stepping forward to use the pitchfork to shove a wayward branch back where it should be. Like two small boys on Guy Fawkes night. Totally content. And oblivious.

Out of the corner of an eye we suddenly noticed a group of largish men running down the lower part of New Mill Lane – the trickiest, steepest part. So there must be something urgent.

It was not until they turned the corner and came down the final slope past the house that we saw they were dragging a hose. Now fire-hydrants are not abundant in New Mill Lane, so they must have connected it to something right up at Caffyn's. Hoses are heavy; and they must have been lugging over three hundred yards of it. You wouldn't think they could get that much on a fire engine. And this wasn't a swish urban unit; this was the Lynton Section, manned, for the most part, by volunteers. Lynton doesn't get that many fires. Well, not like ours.

As the men drew nearer, we saw that they were even bigger than we had estimated when we caught our first sight of them. (I later found out that at least three of them were the sons of a local builder, and the genes had been very generous with the inches.)

After our first bafflement, we next felt rather embarrassed, even though it wasn't our fault. We were simply having a fire in the garden – admittedly a large garden and a large fire. And we were not the ones who had summoned the firemen. They told us that the man who had called them out lived on Dean Steep, between Barbrook and Caffyn's. The tea man, in fact, who had first told me about New Mill. He had been standing outside his back door, thinking of nothing in particular (they do quite a lot of that in North Devon). He couldn't see New Mill from his doorstep, because it was down in the valley. But he could see the smoke, and there was quite a lot of it. He must also have seen some flames reflected against it, which can produce a startling visual effect. He came to the obvious conclusion that our many experiments at starting fires had produced some over-dramatic results. So he did what any good citizen would do: he dialled 999.

They were very good about it, and they cheerfully rolled up their miles of hose with no recriminations. The least we could do was offer them a cup of tea. While Ken was completing negotiations, and apologies, I went into the kitchen to put the kettle on. One by one they came to the door, politely knocked, and were admitted. Again, I marvelled at their size. There were lots of cricked necks as they squeezed in.

There was one still to come. I wondered what was keeping him. Suddenly the light in the room weakened. I looked up. The last man on the threshold was so large that he blocked out the light almost completely. It was like an eclipse of the sun.

A final little postscript to show how fast news spreads in country areas. The firemen must have departed – oooohhh, round about nine or nine-thirty, I suppose. The following morning, at about half-past eight (so only eleven hours later), Joe Pyall brought our post down the hill. His opening gambit was: 'I hear you had a spot of trouble last night then.'

14

Swapping

People must have good reasons for giving up their comfortable semi and moving into a place like New Mill. I think we had the best reason of all: we couldn't think of anything better to do. They say that would-be monks become actual monks not because of any calling, vocation, piety, holiness, or anything else biblical; they do it because they cannot think of anything else. As life presented itself to them, there really was no other decision. They didn't sit down with a list of pro's and con's for several possible callings. They didn't choose the contemplative, remote life; it chose them. At the very least it beckoned to them, and they found it difficult to give serious consideration to other paths. There really was nothing else that showed any sign of practicality and peace.

I am not saying that our move to New Mill had the remotest ingredient of holiness in it – God forbid. (Well, He would have done, wouldn't He?) But it bears some similarity in that it just happened, and in that it seemed the next thing to do. I don't remember agonised family discussions about lists of priorities and likely potential of courses of action. We just did it. It certainly had the merit of avoiding soul-searching or recrimination, much less regret. Much less again the immediate urge to get out of it.

Which is odd, because the life had several features, and presented several problems, which would have put off a lot of people. Make no mistake; we were not made of pioneer stock; we were not bewitched by 'the country'; we did not want 'to get away from it all'. All that made us different was that we were there. Rather like the First World War song: 'We're 'ere because we're 'ere because we're 'ere.'

131

Once you have accepted that, you start to discover all sorts of things that would not have occurred to you beforehand.

Good health, for a start. We lived in a chilly old stone building with no central heating, no double glazing, no metalled road nearer than a quarter of a mile. The water supply for the house came through a long black plastic hose that stretched right up to a spring over fifty yards away. This spring fed into a tiny rivulet which was frequently crossed and sloshed about in by cattle who could be suffering from things like liver fluke. The water we took from this was initially held in a catchment tank made of asbestos, and it gurgled in its plastic pipe across the leet, and through the raspberry canes and the Japanese knotweed. We were raising a new baby. A health visitor today would have a fit. Oddly, Miss Blackmore, our retired health visitor, raised no objection and offered no criticism. Different generation.

Be that as it may, I don't remember anyone being ill. Well, not seriously. Coughs and colds, yes (and very few of those), but nothing dire. Christopher got bitten once by a horse fly, and on another occasion broke a wrist (which he could have done anywhere); Stephen once had a couple of days when he was happy to take to his bed; Martin got nothing at all. Mother had the occasional migraine, and Father copped a bout of 'flu' (from his school, probably; no virus was robust enough to make the trip out to New Mill on its own, so to speak), but migraines and 'flu', like broken wrists, could have happened anywhere.

Wherever we wanted to go – on business, that is – we had to walk up the hill. Very good for the wind and the thigh muscles. Much easier, of course, when I bought the 'new' Land Rover. Not content with that, we would walk out on to Exmoor – Saddle Gate, Woodbarrow, Cheriton Ridge, Badgworthy, the Long Stone, the Hoar Oak Tree – or the other way, over to other resorts near the Bristol Channel – Hunter's Inn, Woody Bay, Martinhoe.

Very soon after our arrival, the BBC launched one of its early historical episodic dramas – about the first Queen Elizabeth. It promised to be good, and I was a History teacher. We had no television (another item on most people's list of indispensables). But a local tradesman, who had already done us several favours, offered to let us come over each week and watch. I can't think now why we didn't use the Mini. Perhaps Mrs. Coates didn't relish the prospect of Devon lanes in the dark (and in the winter), and I hadn't learned to drive yet. So we walked – *walked* – each week for six weeks, from New Mill to Lynton, to see Glenda Jackson in glorious technicolour and a dumbfounding array of outrageously ornate dresses. I don't recall that we thought it any great hardship. I think Miss Blackmore baby-sat for us.

Fresh air, space, strange and unexpected opportunities – it all had the makings of an event factory.

Christopher and Martin discovered a neglected house a mile or two away – Woolhanger – and had some adventures there. Rumour had it that there had been a murder there unmentioned years ago – which added a frisson of mystery, even danger. A ruin, a lake, woods and wilderness, a story of sudden death – what more would boys want? They were welcome visitors at the stables and guest house up the valley, and spent hours in the holidays with the two sons of the family, James and Andrew. Andrew was about Christopher's age. James was two or three years older, and of a resourceful turn of mind, so he became, I presume, the natural leader.

They took it into their heads to make a go-cart, and were delighted to discover, in a field, a piece of old unwanted machinery with a set of iron wheels. The local farmer said they were welcome to it; all they had to do was separate the wheels from the rest. It took them three days with hacksaws to chop off what they wanted. More of the go-cart later.

They once found a dilapidated, time-expired motor scooter – God knows where. Thanks largely, I should think, to the facilities in the stable workshop, and James' precocious mechanical instinct, they got it to work. Of course they could go nowhere near a road, because they were all under age, but on farm tracks and yards nobody seemed to mind. Chances were that nobody knew. I certainly didn't, so had no opportunity to worry about it, much less to moralise about it.

Adventure did not overlook Mrs. Coates: out for a constitutional one morning, with Stephen slung on her hip, she walked up the hill to West Ilkerton, and bumped into the local bull. The encounter had no dimensions of the *corrida* to it. Nevertheless, it is a trifle disconcerting to find such a creature loafing across your path. Like most bulls, and lions, when you catch sight of them, it didn't appear to be doing anything much, but mothers with babies slung on their hips are not inclined to try and persuade such animals to step aside. It was not the time to speculate whether it was benign, totally uninterested, introspective, somnolent, or maybe resting from its labours on the farm. However, despite what the cliché would say, she did not 'beat a hasty retreat'; she had it firmly rooted in her head that bulls like sport, and are fond of a chase if people they bump into start to run. So it was a case of slow, dignified, and very wary, withdrawal, rather like the traditional obsequious lackey leaving the royal presence. She talked about it for years.

We were never short of drama and exercise, it seemed.

Before a year was up, we also encountered an advantage that no prospective inmate of a country cottage would have dreamed of: we were given the choice of a second country cottage.

Stephen was at the bottom of this little saga too. When it became clear that he was, if not imminent, distinctly looming over the horizon, some thinking had to be done. Like most babies, he would stay in with us in the early days, but that wouldn't last for ever. The boys' bedroom was far from spacious. A problem was approaching.

You never know with country cottages, as I have already said several times. The solution came from a most unexpected quarter.

A few months after we had arrived, Ken took a wife too. A second one; he had grown-up children by his first one. Martha, her name was, but I never met her, and Ken hardly ever referred to her. How long they had been divorced I never knew. Ken rarely discussed his private life. But then I didn't discuss mine either.

Anyway, one day, Ken appeared with Elise. Another person with a marriage behind her. Two actually. Unlike Ken, she *did* talk about *them* – rather more than one would have expected someone to do on a fresh acquaintance. Clearly she had had a somewhat colourful career. She couldn't have been more different from Ken. He had some dimensions of the natural bachelor about him; she was a lady of the world – well, two husbands – she would be, wouldn't she? Smart dresser, quick speech and movement, cigarettes, possibly some peroxide in the hair. But lively conversation, plenty to talk *about*, some of it quite racy – she was light years away from Ken. How had they got together?

This throws up another facet of Ken's personality, which often puzzled us. He was, as I hope I have conveyed, no Douglas Fairbanks and no heart-throb, yet he never failed to display a gift for acquiring the company of women. Jumping ahead for a moment – after he and Elise divorced (well, they would; it was never going to work), and after we had left New Mill, we saw him from time to time, and he was never without female company. Nice ladies too. I stress the 'ladies'. My abiding memory of Ken is baggy, empire-builder's shorts, beaky nose, hands calloused with oil and hard work, and a slightly absent air. How did he do it?

Elise, to her credit, accepted New Mill, and seemed to enjoy the time she spent there. Perhaps she saw it as an opportunity to provide space and entertainment for a daughter she brought with her – Pollyanna. I think she was the offspring of her second husband. But that is no matter. She had clearly been brought up most of the time by Elise, and she no doubt learned to adjust to her mother's way of living. Like her mother, she was not short of self-confidence. And for a ten-year-old – once more like her mother – she gave an impression of awareness; you felt that she knew more than a normal ten-year-old did – or should.

She fastened on to Martin, who had never met anybody like her in his life. His had been a quiet suburban existence. Because of his tongue-tie, he wasn't the greatest conversationalist in the world. Perhaps in turn because of that he tended to more solitary pastimes. True, he played with Christopher, and, later, with Stephen, but his natural inclinations were not gregarious. His life, when left to himself, was made up of Lego, gadgets, and wires.

It was a curious repetition of Ken and Elise. Unworldliness and sophistication. Deliberation and capricious energy. Pollyanna simply took Martin over; he was cannon fodder for her. She was all initiative; he was all disciple. We still talk of the time we saw them going past the front door, Pollyanna a yard or two in the lead, with a set jaw of determination clearly in evidence; Martin obediently in the wake. In fact not obediently; it was helplessly. As he went by, he looked at us and sort of shrugged. He was in the grip of a power and personality bigger than his own resources could cope with. He didn't seem in the least unhappy. Just hypnotised. Behind the Pied Piper of Hamelin.

Martin was lost to us all, rather like Toad with motor-cars. Maybe this might partly explain why Christopher took up fishing; he was, albeit temporarily, seeing less of his brother.

It didn't last, as I said. I believe Elise took off in the end. What happened to Posie (that's what her mother called her) I can only speculate. If she collected a husband or two on the way, I shouldn't be a bit surprised.

However, it was Elise who came up with the bright idea I was talking about. It was clear to all that our bedroom situation was not going to get any better. I suppose it may have occurred to Ken that we might take steps towards a move of house. I don't say that our modest rent made all the difference between affluence and penury for him, but, though I say so myself, I was making a contribution towards the Great New Mill Development Project. My limited knowledge, and (now that I was working full-time in Barnstaple) my narrower opportunities to do much in the way of physical improvement, were not taking us appreciably, or fast, nearer to the 'Roses Round the Door' idyllic vision that bewitches most people in their pipe dreams.

However, we (the whole family) were simply there – all the time. I doubt very much whether the contents of New Mill (auction sale furniture and ancient horse brasses) presented any irresistible temptation to would-be burglars. Even if they did, how would they have got rackety wardrobes and ancient bedsprings up New Mill Lane when they would have been unlikely to get a van *down* New Mill Lane? And how they could have asked David Leworthy to bring his tractor and cart along to assist in housebreaking? There is a lot to be said for making your possessions unenviable.

More prosaically, I think we simply kept the place running, aired, and lived in. All houses need that. Ken was still tied to his terms at Bristol Tech. and his other labours in Iron Acton. So – yes – we were useful.

Elise, the newcomer, could see things more simply and starkly than the regular occupants. She took one look at the whole of New Mill, and said, in effect, 'Why not change ends?'

Why not indeed? Ken and Elise were living in the larger half – two reception rooms as against one, plus a large hall. They were only two; we were four – soon to be five. The one was as ramshackle and half-done as the other. The same facilities (or lack of facilities) applied in both. Same stone floors, same toilet (literally – we shared it for a while till Ken completed our bathroom); same dependence on outside gas cylinders, and so on. It came down in effect to a question of space. Nevertheless, it was a generous offer, and we could do no other but thank him.

We arranged a long weekend – well, three days. I contracted a mysterious sudden cold on the Monday, which kept me away from work till Tuesday. And we went to work. Thank God it wasn't raining.

As for the benefits and shortcomings, they were what you might expect, with a place like New Mill. There was always a kick-back.

For example, I was not sorry to see the back of our front door (if you see what I mean), with its low lintel (the one the firemen had to squeeze through by bending like the Hunchback of Notre Dame). But, in the new half, I was soon painfully aware that the lintel from the lounge to the hall was even lower. No matter how hard you to try to remember, if you're deep in a household task, you forget – till it hits you. Even if you are moving at an indoor walk from A to B, it is amazing how much momentum you generate. More than once I hit my head so hard that I fell back to the floor.

The doorway from the lounge to the kitchen was not exactly lofty either. In the other half there was no doorway at all – so no discomfort in moving around.

The fireplace in Ken's lounge was of course much bigger, almost majestic. With its much-talked-of bread oven. It is amazing how many owners of large fireplaces feel compelled to tell one and all about their bread oven. I know; we used to do it ourselves. It was a 'great feature', and a definite, unmistakable sign that the cottage was 'traditional'. It was like having a loom and a spinning wheel in the corner.

Yet that oven was never opened – well, not for business. We peered inside once or twice, but all we got was an impression of dust and rust. So we never did anything about it.

The only bit of old iron that was useful (apart from a score of savage-looking hooks rammed into the outside walls, which were useful for hanging buckets on – perhaps they were used originally for chaining up arrested poachers) was a huge slab which was propped against the wall behind the fire. It was yet another trophy which Ken had prised out of a closed-house auction. But it did the job; it could throw out the heat.

The fire was hard work. It was so much bigger than the other one, and so used up more fuel. It seemed to scatter ash over a wider area. Another snag it was to present was the need to protect a wandering infant. The fireguard we had to buy was enormous. However, the whole unit was much better behaved than the 'Harry Smokers' antique in the old lounge. It allowed you to enjoy the *smell* of woodsmoke; in the old half you were too often coughing and spluttering to get around to sniffing. There is something devilish attractive about woodsmoke. Or perhaps not so much attractive as evocative. It conjures up much more in the imagination than a dozen bread ovens.

15

Comparing

Half-past seven on a dark, chill January morning. Up at Caffyn's Cross, to catch the 310 single-decker to Barnstaple. (So it really meant the alarm clock set for six.) Dismount at the Bus Station, walk through the town, up through Rock Park, alongside the River Taw, up Park Lane (there's a misnomer for you), and turn right into Barnstaple Grammar School.

Compare that with a leisurely stroll through the Fairfield – all of five minutes – to Kingston Grammar School, where I worked for nearly twelve years.

Classes for History, English – and more classes for History and English – going on for ever. New school; new staff; new pupils (of course); new rooms and corridors; new everything. The head span. The nervous energy required to deal with each of them was prodigious. I cannot remember a longer morning; I was exhausted before we sat down to lunch.

Compare that with Year 12 work on 'A' Level History, a couple of English classes, and a Year 9 top stream History group, plus three or four afternoons each week out on the Games field.

Oh, yes, and I was also given a Year 13 (Upper Sixth as was) for the two remaining terms of the 'A' Level syllabus. When I was offered the job, the Headmaster asked me if I had experience of 'A' Level English. I said of course I knew all about 'A' Level English. Well, if you wanted the job that badly, wouldn't you? Luckily, the Headmaster wanted me that badly too, and, whatever his suspicions were, he wisely did not ask me to elaborate. Well, I thought, History wasn't all that different from English Literature, and 'A' Level was 'A'

Level, wasn't it? When we practise to deceive, we do indeed weave a tangled web for other people, but we weave one even worse for ourselves.

Many bus journeys in the following weeks were taken up with discovering what lay between the covers of *As You Like It*, *Selected Poems of Thomas Hardy*, and James Joyce's *Portrait of the Artist as a Young Man*. A far cry from William Pitt's foreign policy.

Ironically, nobody asked me if I had any experience of taking Games. I really did know something about that, but thought carefully before opening my mouth. The Army had taught me never to volunteer for anything. I had spent nearly twelve years coaching hockey through every winter and cricket through every summer. Here was a Heaven-sent opportunity. Anyway, I did feel that I had done my whack, and I now had a family to occupy my weekends, so I felt no conscience about it.

So it wasn't only New Mill that produced a series of shocks. As with New Mill too, the shocks kept on coming.

First up was to secure my employment. The Head had told me from the outset that the job was purely as a supply teacher. Admittedly a long-term supply teacher, but supply nevertheless. The permanent post would be advertised to commence in the following September, and interviews would take place in the summer. I had six months to prove myself, and then apply for my own job.

Luckily I did. But I knew from experience that no considerations of justice would have counted for much. I thought I was the best candidate, but that need not mean a thing, as I was later to discover on more than one occasion. So, I repeat, it was as much luck as anything.

Well, I had a job. A year later I was made Head of History. And I suspect that that was not necessarily explained by virtue or justice. The previous head of history had gone off to the local tech. to do the same up there, and the next in line was terminally ill. Not much of a qualification, is it – just to be left around. I was also asked to take charge of the subject of General Studies for the entire Sixth Form.

140

Here was another depressing prospect. Nobody *likes* General Studies, either staff or pupils. It is a non-subject. It is just something that well-meaning educationists (who always know best) thought would be good for you, like having a 'flu' jab in winter. So I had a bolshy sixth form. Round about that time, the local authority had decreed that Barnstaple Grammar School was to be wiped out, and a comprehensive school put in its place. Imagine the bruised feelings about that. The Headmaster (a new headmaster, as luck would have it) was left with a lame duck academic institution under sentence of death, and everybody concerned was facing the problem of how to get through the next two years before the body was buried (and not even decently). The Head later admitted to me that, no matter how much effort I was to put into arranging classes for a sixth-form General Studies course, it was going to be merely a holding operation. All in all, not encouraging.

However, it did get better. As a head of department, I was now able to call some shots. The 'A' Level History syllabus was pretty much the same as I had had to deal with at Kingston. I had all my evenings and weekends – no after-school nets and practices; no hours travelling and umpiring. For my first bash at General Studies, the master in charge (this was before I took over) gave me a dozen or so, to do drama. I could do anything I liked.

The trouble was, there was only one boy in the group. There are not many plays around for a single male and a near-monopoly of female parts. I had a bright idea, born of desperation. I tackled the solitary boy, who, as it happened, was genuinely interested in acting. I said, 'If I do the trial scene from Shaw's *St. Joan* , would you be willing to do Joan and have all the girls as the inquisitors?' To my great relief, he said yes.

So we did it. The girls relished the idea of being the masterful ones who put the only male in his place (even it was at the stake), and the boy produced a really sensitive and un-self-conscious performance. At any rate, it held the rest of the Sixth Form, who were rounded up to watch it being performed.

As a means of closing, I arranged for a telescoping of events (another necessity), and had Joan taken offstage, straight to the fire. The back-stage boys arranged some suitable flickering lights and crackling noises. I had taken one of the girls on one side a few days before, carefully choosing the bustiest one, stood her in front of a recording mike, and told her to scream her head off. What with the flames, the crackling, the silent figures of the inquisitors listening on a darkened stage to the results of their verdict, and the crazed operatic agonies recorded from the wings, it produced quite an effect. Well, at any rate, they listened in total silence. There was no fidgeting and groping for their bags and books.

One last little oddity was concerned with scenery. Put simply, I didn't have any. And no budget. No costumes either.

I repaired therefore to the Poor Clares convent in Lynton, to ask if I could borrow some of the nuns' habits. All black and flowing – ideal. I was told to wait in a small room, one wall of which was taken up with a long steel grille, with mesh intervals like those in chicken wire, only much stronger. After a suitable delay, the door behind the grille opened, and a nun appeared, sat down exactly opposite me, and asked me my business.

She didn't look very old; it turned out that she was the Mother Superior. A jolly, sociable soul too. We talked about convents, and Lynton, and recent politics, and schools, and I don't know what. When I put my request, she fell in with it remarkable willingness. And with interest too.

The Poor Clares normally wore brown habits, and I asked if by chance they had any black ones.

'Oh, yes,' she said. 'We often wear them underneath the brown ones. See.'

To my consternation and near-disbelief, she bent down and lifted the hem of her own habit to prove it. If, before my visit, I had been told that the Mother Superior of the local convent would show a total stranger a glimpse of her underclothes, I would have laughed, or worse, have uttered a monosyllabic expletive of scorn. But that's what she did. Scouts' honour, that's what she did.

One last little touch, of holy privacy. She had asked me to give them a day or so to prepare the clothes. When I went back to get them, she did not hand them to me. In the corner, at the end of the grille, was a compartment with a sliding mechanism. She put the clothes in on her side and shut the door on it. She slid the machinery round, and the door appeared on my side. I opened it, and there they all were, neatly done up – a dozen black habits.

That dealt with the costume dimension. It left scenery. The school hall was one of many, all over the country, I should guess, which did not have a permanent stage. Instead, at one end were numerous large black wooden platforms, each about six feet square. These could be arranged in a variety of patterns in order to produce the required elevation (about eighteen inches high – or more if you stacked them double) for the players, visitors, celebrities who might need to be up on view. A sort of stage Lego.

So I stood some of them on end, at odd angles, and suggested therefore that we were dealing with forbidding black walls suitable for a court of inquisition. For the lofty, imposing court bench, I stacked them.

Apparently, it worked. The teacher then in charge of General Studies had invited the county drama adviser to come and see it. He was very taken with it all. What freedom – reversal of the sexes. What drama – the sound effects, the telescoping of events, the screaming. Above all the impressive scenery – what fertile originality. He invited me to join the local dramatic society.

I hadn't the heart to tell him I was no prodigiously creative *wunderkind* who aspired to topple Peter Hall from the RSC. It had all come about simply because I was desperate. I certainly didn't fancy risking the unmasking of my limitations by joining the local dram. soc.

In 1972 came the big challenge for everybody: the local authority had decided to abolish grammar schools and go comprehensive. So Barnstaple Grammar was to shut down, and it, and the local secondary modern school, were to be reborn as 11-16 comprehensives. Every pupil over 16 was to be accommodated at what was known as 'the Tech', and which, to give the flavour of dignity and academic excellence, was to be renamed as 'The North Devon College'. Same place. Bit bigger, of course. But the same place.

This had obviously been in the wind for some time, and many of the old Grammar School staff had sought academic teaching elsewhere. Some old staff stayed on, for the usual variety of reasons – loyalty, habit, age, wariness. The new ones were the mixture you might have expected, and I have no doubt that they were selected with the new all-ability population in mind. Rightly so.

The 'grammar-school' types who stayed on found themselves not only out of fashion but out of favour. Suddenly many of their qualifications and attitudes were under the critical eye of the new establishment – the pioneers. Nobody actually said anything, but it became clear that there was a definite new climate of opinion: it was high time these toffee-nosed grammar school teachers forgot their precious academic niceties; it was high time they realised that the kids they had been teaching hitherto were a privileged minority; it was high time they had some real teaching to do, with proper children. Time, as it was said, that they joined the real world.

Well, that is as may be. But my experience was that these traditional academic teachers did what they had always done, and had been trained to do: they mastered their material; they prepared their lessons; they marked the homework; they kept order; they did the job; and they delivered the goods. They worked to extract from each child what they thought that child was capable of. That child's ability was irrelevant; it was what you *did* with that ability that mattered.

It was hard, yes. But teaching is hard anyway. Anyone who thinks it isn't should try it for a term or two. Take it from me: the old grammar-school teachers more than held their own. Indeed, when certain classes began to emerge displaying above-average disciplinary troubles, guess who was often put in charge of them.

This is not a plea for grammar-school style teaching or teachers as such. The comps. soon threw up staff without grammar-school experience who became shining examples in their profession. I am simply making the point that a good teacher is a good teacher, and there were rather more from the grammar schools than the grammar schools were given credit for by the new regime, and that they tackled the new problems produced in the comps. with the same dedication and common sense that they had shown in the grammar schools. They were what they were; they could not have done otherwise.

Of course it was not the same as the grammar schools; if it had been, there would have no point in changing the system. Class sizes were often larger, for example. The new philosophy of mixed ability was much trumpeted. 'Streaming' became a dirty word. Tradition took a knock, because the new comps. didn't have any; they had just been born. Local council estates produced a far higher percentage of criminals than any grammar school would have had to deal with – or would have been *prepared* to deal with. (But that was to change. Not even the comps., in the end, were willing to tolerate *everybody*. Children were removed. It was only a question of vocabulary: grammar schools expelled them; comps. 'excluded' them. It came down to the same thing. 'Special units' were set up to deal with them.)

So there was a lot to learn and a lot to do. No great harm in that. If I had stayed at the grammar school, the chances are that I would have continued in the same furrow until I could hardly see out over the edges. Hardly surprising; it was so agreeable.

Was it all disagreeable then in the comp? No, of course not. Yes, there were some criminals; about five per cent of the pupil population accounted for about ninety-five per cent of the crime rate. There were some misfits, some oddballs. Don't forget that we were only just beginning to become acquainted with concepts like dyslexia, dyspraxia, autism, attention deficiency, and all manner of other '-isms'. There were the usual truants; we called it 'mitching' round our way. Or maybe 'miching'. It was one of those words that were only spoken; you never saw them in print.

There were far more family difficulties that we had been used to in the grammar schools – drink, crime (professional crime, or at any rate habitual crime), child-beating (or worse – we didn't call it 'abuse' in those days; word fashions change). Family relationships, in a closely-lived-in council estate, could become like a bed of nettles; the more you pulled up, the more you discovered – second marriages, second families, half-brothers and sisters (again, you didn't call them 'siblings' then), live-in lovers, 'uncles', common law bastards, cousins once removed, boy friends who ran away with their girl friend's mother. There was always something new on the horizon. You were often lost in amazement at the resilience of some of these children.

What often made it difficult for these boys and girls, the ones who may have yearned for a normal life (because they could see evidence of it at school – they were not stupid), was that the family expectations were so low. If Mum and Dad had had a poor education, it was natural (though maybe not praiseworthy) for them to have no respect for learning as such. Inverted snobbery could be just as powerful a force as the real thing. Desire for academic improvement could be stifled by the fear of having to leave the social environment known since birth. Devonians don't move much, and many of those that do come back later.

Then again, many of these parents had not had a happy school experience themselves. School had become a foreign place. Teachers were 'authority'- the powers that be – *them*. Any child born into this milieu would have found it difficult to think any other way.

At the same time there was a large number of very nice children (perhaps luckier), who were properly brought up to be respectful and do their best. They were a delight.

One became acquainted with a new world of interests and loyalties. Farming families, for instance, produced different attitudes, habits, even modes of speech (see Chapter 17). It was no good getting cross if some of them took time off for the County Show; this could the biggest event in the farming year. Don't expect much homework to come in during the week of the Barnstaple Fair.

I learned a whole directory of new Christian names. Oddly, it was the council estates who produced the most exotic ones – Vincent, Francis, Nicola. Hundreds of Sharons, Tracys, and Deborahs, of course. Waynes and Shanes too.

The surnames, as I was to discover, reeked of Devon – Beer,

Dallyn, Crocombe, Woollacott, Wonnacott, Tithecott, Brayley, Woodger, Pile, Lock. And half the girls were going to marry somebody with a name in a list like this.

The new life then was, somewhat surprisingly, quite harmonious. The New Mill domestic life fitted with the working life. Both were new; both were quite hard, at any rate to begin with. Both produced surprise, variety, challenge, and shock. Both made demands on character, inventiveness, imagination, patience, and the capacity for tenacity. Both had their moments. Both have figured prominently in my reminiscences ever since, so they must have made a deep impression.

If one had to offer a single word to summarise their joint contribution, I suppose it might be simply 'change'. Life, looking back, had gone cosy and predictable. I was in near-total control. That did not mean that I had no desires and aspirations; it did not mean that I had no moods when I wanted to get the hell out of Kingston, even get the hell out of teaching. But, as far as the working of the job was concerned, I was in as near total control as one had any right to expect. It was all very tolerable.

But New Mill and the new school (and a new family for that matter) changed all that. I did not consciously seek out the sort of life I had in the eight years I spent at New Mill, but that was how it turned out, and that was what, whether I liked it or not, I had to deal with.

The shake-up probably did me good. It was a bit like joining the Army.

16

Meeting Even More

'"'Tis thick up auver.'

In a later chapter, I intend to discuss the business of the Devon accent. By the time you get to the end of it, you may be forgiven for wondering whether I think there is a Devon accent or not, because I quote evidence for either conclusion.

For instance, one could refer to the radio, which introduced us to 'BBC English'. One could mention the dominance of television, which has to be constructed to appeal to as wide a viewing audience as possible. A nation-wide, uniform education service, with its exam syllabuses and 'correct' English, is no friend to local dialect.

On the other hand, you can come across, without warning or preamble, a word or phrase which hits you between the eyes, or rather ears, and which is Devon to the core, and which shows you that 'Deb'm' is alive and kicking.

Despite its modest size, Barbrook, a mile and a half from New Mill, boasted a respectably-sized garage and filling-station. One morning, I was there filling up, or just gossiping. Both Fred and John Hoyles, father and son, like most Devonians, were happy to exchange a spot of gossip – mostly about the weather. Fred drove the early-morning school bus to the primary school, so we got to know him quite quickly, as we put the boys on board every morning. John ran the garage end of it. Later, I believe, he became the Mayor of Lynton.

Anyway, we were standing around talking of this and that. There was a good deal of fog on Exmoor that chill day, so naturally we spoke about it. High ground, naturally, attracted the fog (though

I know that low ground could too; the fingers of autumn mist creeping up river valleys of an evening could be evocative sights). As we did, another vehicle drove up, a local got out, and said to everybody and nobody in particular what most people always said, 'All right, then?' Before anybody could answer, he followed it up with the verdict: ' 'Tis thick up auver.'

No prizes for translating it. And the speaker gets no prizes for originality or Shavian wit. But, coming as and when it did, it was so striking, neat, succinct, relevant, and natural – all in four words. Nobody could have done better. Over forty years later, it is as fresh as if I had heard it yesterday.

Does that make the man who said it a 'character'? No. I said only one thing about him for a start. For another, I didn't know him from Adam. For a third, he was not saying anything that he had not said a thousand times before.

You have to be careful when you write a book like this. It doesn't do to write self-consciously about 'characters'. It's like all writing; you don't take the reader by the scruff of the neck and bully him into accepting that you are describing a mood or an atmosphere or a personality. Ideally, what you should do is to collect enough fact and impression to convey a certain truth (as you see it), and hope that the reader will decide for himself that this event was 'dramatic' or that happening was 'remarkable' or the person you describe was a 'character'. You can only hope for the best.

I have always been suspicious of people who move to 'the country' and describe their new life as if they are permanent tourists among a population of 'characters'. When you *live* somewhere, it isn't like that. You are still yourself, however hard you may claim to live like the natives. All you can do is to mind your manners and your own business, and trust that it will do. That you will be accepted instead of being merely tolerated.

One of the tell-tale marks of this is the over-use of Christian names. It can become, at the best, rather forward, and at the worst patronising. One example from a later period, when we had moved from New Mill and into a village near Barnstaple. Our local butcher's name was Elliott. So we always called him 'Mr. Elliott'. This went on for years. One day, I was in there and ordering our pork chops or hog's pudding, and minding my manners, and he suddenly said, 'Mr. Coates [correct, you see, and I was a customer], you have been coming in here for a long time. Don't you think it's about time you called me "Dudley"?'

I came home, dumped the hog's pudding triumphantly on the kitchen table, and said, 'I have arrived. After seventeen years, I have arrived. I have been given permission to address our butcher by his Christian name.' It was worth the wait. By no stretch could I have been accused of being patronising, and that was very satisfying.

But there were many others whose Christian name we never got around to. Fred Leworthy, for a start. I have called him 'Fred' in this book, but I would never have used it to his face. Miss Blackmore was always 'Miss Blackmore' – never 'Dorothy' (and certainly not 'Doth', which was her family name). The senior figures in Richards and Rumbelows were always 'Mr. Richards' and 'Mr Rumbelow'. Keith and Ron, the respective sons, were our own age, even perhaps younger, so it was easier with them.

All of which is getting away, perhaps, from the theme of the chapter – describing more of the people with whom we became acquainted. I mention them not because they are 'characters', but because they said or did things which stuck in the memory. There must have been many people around us who never found their way there. Just as we talk fondly about the great Hollywood films of the old days, as if they made nothing but great ones. We don't talk about the majority – which were routine, everyday, mundane, and totally unmemorable potboilers. Of course it is arguable that the people we do talk about must have had character-potential or they *wouldn't* have stuck in the memory. Or again, perhaps their role in this book is to add to the composite picture of a community which *had* 'character' rather than *was* a 'character' in their own right, as it were.

Take Mrs. Hildick. All I can really tell you about her is summed up in the word 'cake'. She ran a bakery and confectionery beside the bus station in Lynton. Ken found her originally; I didn't. She was a kindly and friendly lady, and, shall we say, 'of mature years'. I never saw her outside her bakery, so I always think of her wearing a garment which was half overall and half apron. Like many Devonians, ready for a chat. Her tea-shop was never exactly thronged with customers, so she usually had some time to spare.

What was so special about her then? I'll tell you what was special about her: she made the most sensational slab cake that you would find in the length and breadth of the kingdom.

A lovely mature colour for the top. Just the right number of currants or sultanas. Too many and it becomes a cheap form of Christmas cake. Too few and it's doughy and chewy. Sugar level spot on. Not too damp and not too dry. Substantial in both texture and thickness; you knew you were eating something. Like Baby Bear's porridge, it was just right.

I'm sorry, but I can't do better than that. You will just have to take my word for it. Whenever Ken and I went into Lynton, we always tried to make time for a cup of tea at Mrs. Hildick's and a paving stone of her slab cake. I have never eaten slab cake since which comes anywhere near it.

Tiny images: the lady in the dairy, of substantial content and serious mien, and whose name was Lorna. (There's another one whose Christian name I would never have dreamed of using to her face.) This was *Lorna Doone* country, remember, and Lorna was the slender, nubile, smiling heroine of a treasured story. This lady was, I'm sure, kind and efficient, but her name simply did not 'sit' very well with her. It wasn't any fault of hers; it was our wilful imagination. Very unfair.

There was a tiny little haberdashery near Fred Fouracre's butcher's shop. In these days of mass-grocery and online purchase, I doubt whether it would survive five minutes now, but, then, it ticked over very nicely under the single-handed, genteel, very ladylike governance of Dulcie Murley. The very name 'Dulcie' conjured it up. She sang madrigals with the local choir.

At the other end of town, up on the main road, near the universal corner shop which sold absolutely everything for the visitors from picture postcards to buckets and spades and the local paper, was a tailor. Not just any old tailor; this one made garments out of sheepskins. Real bespoke sheepskin. Pretty rare, I should think – though perhaps they were more numerous in places like Australia and Lapland and Sweden. (Sweden seems an unlikely place for growing sheep, but I read a book recently about a chap who lived a rustic life in Spain, but who, in order to pay his way, used to travel to Sweden every winter to shear sheep.)

I couldn't afford the great big jackets, but I did push the boat out with a Russian-style fur-trimmed hat. Very Slavonic. Straight out of *War and Peace* and the Retreat from Moscow. But I had to make do without a *droshky*.

At a party in Lynton I met a man with whom I reminisced about the War. I told him that I had been evacuated to North Devon to escape the Blitz. He was a bit older than that; it turned out that he had been old enough to join the Home Guard. But only just; he claimed that he was the original Private Pike.

In the early seventies, there was a general election. This was the period of strikes, of power cuts, of the wicked Arabs raising the price of their oil (dashed unsporting), and of the Edward Heath three-day week. The MP for Lynton was a man called Jeremy Thorpe. Those with short memories today might say, 'Jeremy who?' But, in his day, he really was a 'character', because he set out to be one – Oxford, the bar, public speaker, double-breasted grey waistcoats, precocious promotion to leadership of the Liberal party, coming within a whisker of attaining Cabinet participation for a minority party, and general gift for notoriety.

There was allegedly a piece of newsreel on view which showed him parading through the streets of Lynton, on some kind of victory progress. He was waving his arms in triumph and delighting in acknowledging the plaudits of the packed pavements. But the camera was on him alone. There was hardly anybody on the pavements. An outrageous piece of theatre, which, true or not, seemed right up his street. This is such an evocative image that today I can conjure it up clearly in the mind's eye. It comes back so easily that I have to admit that am not sure whether it has been translated in my mind from story to fact, or whether I actually did see it.

There was a mystery about Jeremy Thorpe. In fact there were several. His first wife was sadly killed in an unusual road accident, on her own. He had a somewhat prominent monument to her erected on top of Codden Hill in Bishop's Tawton (where he lived), from which you could see for miles. Later he married an ex-countess who, before that, had been a concert pianist. She later nursed him for years when he became ill with Parkinson's.

He was involved in a much-publicised scandal story, in which he was supposed to have had a relationship with a man called Norman Scott. It was even more publicised later when he was investigated for having plotted the removal of this Mr. Scott. The charges were conspiracy and incitement to murder. Which seems a mite drastic for a politician who had only lost a parliamentary seat and who wore double-breasted waistcoats. You don't get politicians being charged with conspiracy and incitement to murder every day of the week. The story was meat and drink to the tabloids.

It came to trial. The judge dismissed it because he said there was no case to answer. It seemed a little odd (another mystery), considering that the police must have been doubly cautious about bringing such a charge against such a celebrity (and a barrister), and should have amassed an impressive folio of evidence, if only to avoid a counter-charge for wrongful arrest. Yet not only was he acquitted; the judge said there was no case to answer.

It seems inescapable that there must have been something that we were not told. You felt that a small effort on the part of *somebody* would have cleared the record once and for all, but for some reason nobody did. It is not for me to insinuate one way or the other. Mr. Thorpe is as likely to have been innocent as he was to have been guilty, from what we know. It is a pity, if only for his own sake, and that of his long-suffering wife, that the case was never cleared up.

If it was in fact cleared up, and I am therefore a gullible member of the public who is naively ignorant of facts which sophisticated or moderately informed people treat as common knowledge, then I can only apologise for that ignorance, but that was how it struck me at the time.

Not long ago, the public were regaled with a dramatic (and remarkably frank and explicit) re-creation of the whole affair. Indeed the suggestive word 'affair' appeared in the title. So we all had a much more accessible opportunity to form, or revise, our own impressions.

Another chance remark echoes clearly down the years. It came from a man I had never seen before and was never to see again. He was a Welsh coalman – well, the driver of a lorry laden with coal.

There was a coal yard at the back of the bus station car park, behind Mrs. Hildick's cake shop. This Welshman had just delivered a load of coal. Ordinary enough. But it appeared that his journey had taken him right across the north of Somerset and Devon, presumably from a Welsh coal mine.

That route is hilly. In fact it boasts not one of the most notorious steep gradients in the country, but three – Porlock, Countisbury, and Lynmouth. Porlock in fact is so notorious that it has had a limerick written about it:

A novice was driving a car,
When, down Porlock, his son said , 'Papa,
If you drive at this rate,
We are bound to be late.
Drive faster.' He did. And they are.

The cliffside at Countisbury, so it is claimed, constitutes the steepest and furthest sheer drop in the country. The road over Countisbury Hill climbs to well over a thousand feet.

Lynmouth has sinister emergency sand-filled run-offs to the left of the road, obviously put there to snatch to safety careless or unlucky drivers who suddenly find themselves out of control. Even the drop from the main Lynton-Barnstaple road into the town has gradients and bends which command care and respect.

So it is quite a place.

This man arrived in the coal yard in a state of nerves amounting almost to shock. He had, he said, a lot of experience in steering coal lorries up and around hills and valleys in Wales, but he had never come across anything like the terrible triple threat – Porlock, Countisbury, and Lynmouth. Never again, he swore.

He would have described his journey as 'epic', no doubt, but its epic potential would have been dwarfed by the episode which had taken place in 1899, and which has become as integral to the history of Lynmouth, Countisbury, and Porlock as the story of Lady Godiva has become to Coventry.

The drama began on the evening of 12th January, 1899, when news reached the Lynmouth Post Office that a ship was in danger of drifting ashore in heavy rain and fierce wind off Porlock. The nearest station, Watchet, could not launch its lifeboat because of the storm. So it was the Lynmouth lifeboat or nothing. But the boat could not be launched from there either. So it was decided to drag the lifeboat, all the way from Lynmouth to Porlock, to be launched from the sheltered harbour there. By road. Thirteen miles. With horse and human muscle. Up the 1 in 4½ hill at Countisbury, down the 1 in 4 hill at Porlock. A vehicle (boat and carriage) weighing ten tons. In the dark.

And they did it. And the boat in distress was saved.

We know the names of the whole crew. Naturally – they are legendary by now. Look at them – Richards, Moore, Ridler, Burgess, Crocombe, Crick, Jarvis, Pennicott, Pugsley, Rawle, Ward (there were brothers and cousins there). I have taught children with these names. They are the quintessence of North Devon.

One of these names has figured in our lives at New Mill, but for another reason – Crocombe.

David Crocombe was a mason. Devon grows a lot of stone. So it also grows a lot of masons. Take a look at any sizeable walls as you go around Devon (well, North Devon at least – that's the bit I know); they are always impressive – what you feel walls ought to look like.

Ken hired the services of David Crocombe when he needed skilled assistance with the building of his septic tank and filter bed.

It was the first Easter I spent at New Mill, and, unusually, it was a scorcher, and we had taken on a big job. It did not bother David. He went about it at what seemed a steady, deliberate walk, and the breeze blocks were charmed into place almost while you were not looking. You'd feel confident that he would have gone about it in exactly the same way if he had been building the Great Wall of China.

He was a tall, rangy fellow, about thirty-ish, I suppose. Obviously well trained, because he did a lot of varied work for both Ken and me in the succeeding years, and nothing seemed to faze him.

For example, I once did some labouring and fetching and carrying for him in a summer holiday. He was mending a roof in the nearby village of Parracombe. The house was tall and the roof was steep. I spent two or three days up there with him, knee deep in roof battens and tiles and black roofing felt. As my steeplejackery was a bit rusty, I spent most of my time up there hanging on by every hand and foot available. David just walked up and down, balancing on the cross-battens, as if he were strolling round the garden. I can't imagine now how I ever came to be involved in the business. The mouth goes dry now at the mere thought.

Not only was he going about his work with total disregard (it seemed) for the risks which were screaming at me; he kept up a constant flow of conversation and reminiscence which seemed inexhaustible. Some of it could be so absorbing that you would almost forget where you were – right up there.

As he told his stories, he would pause frequently to gaze into space. I thought at first that he was simply trying to remember a name or something, or was swallowing his saliva before picking up the story again. But the pauses were longer than that, almost uncomfortable. It was as if he had switched off. Then, just as you were beginning to look for further tell-tale signs of incipient dementia, he would look up at you and say, 'Yeh!' As if to say, 'I assure you it is true, and I hope you are paying attention.'

It was a bit like Ken's incessant humming; with both of them you were kept on pins waiting for the next few bars or the next 'Yeh!'

If the story was particularly involved, his voice – quite soft actually, and a light tenor – would rise steadily with each dramatic revelation. The really good yarns could produce a range, you felt, of two or three octaves.

From what he said, you gathered that he must have been no angel, either as a schoolboy or as an apprentice. But he could tell a story against himself. Apparently, one morning he was at the foot of a ladder, mixing cement for his mason, who was up the ladder, doing some pointing or something. David was having a great time making deliberate mistakes, going slow, keeping his man waiting for the next consignment of fresh cement, and generally being a bloody nuisance. His man up the ladder had had enough. Without warning, he waited for David to deliver the next tray of fresh cement, held it till David was half-way back down again and then tipped the entire contents straight on to his head. 'Yeh!' Even David admitted that it taught him a lesson.

Then there was the Vernon saga. Vernon was a regular mate that he worked with. Vernon, it appears, was a good-looking, well-set-up young fellow, and a bit of a lad with the ladies. On one job they were working at, a young lady in a house on the other side of the road seemed to give him a lot of her attention – pausing for gossip, hanging around her front gate pretending to do some gardening, peering rather too frequently out of her front window.

Vernon, as was his habit in such matters, was quick on the uptake. David warmed to his theme.

'An' Vern said, "Joo know what? She faancies me." [David's voice began to rise.]

'And joo know what'e did? 'E wen' 'crahs the rowd and knocked on 'er dawerr. . . . Yeh! An' when she come to the dawerr, Vern said, bold as braass, ' "Joo faancy me?" [Another half-octave jump.] 'An' she said, "Yes." An' 'e wen' in. Jus' like thaat. [Up nearly to top C.] Yeh!'

We must tear ourselves away from Vernon's amatory exploits, because the rest of the story requires little imagination, and because I should like to finish with David's venture into the Big City – London.

He and a couple of mates – all Devon boys – decided that they were going to have a great day in the capital, visiting some big exhibition – Olympia – somewhere like that. Well, they made it to Paddington all right. The next leg of the journey was, obviously, on the Tube. They made the best they could out of the escalator, found the train, fairly empty as it happened, and sat down like shy patients in a fearsome doctor's waiting-room.

It seemed rather a long way, and they peered at the diagrams on the angle between the windows and the ceiling. They got no joy out of that. At last, by good luck, an inspector came through the carriage, and they asked him when they were going to get to Olympia.

'How long have you been on this train?' he said with screwed-up eyes.

They told him.

'Do you know which line you are on?

They didn't know. He told them.

'This is the Inner Circle; you must have been right round three times by now.'

Yeh!

17

Speaking and Listening

One aspect of the Great Cottage Dream which bemuses most of us is to do with language. Even those of us who suffer from the dream in its acutest form know that we are not going actually to learn another language. But we do look forward to making the acquaintance of another culture, known loosely, to would-be escapers from city and suburb, as 'The Country'. Part of that new culture is the way people speak.

So we are going to rub shoulders with new neighbours with a new idiom, new pronunciation, new vocabulary, and a set of vowel sounds and grammatical constructions (or rather ungrammatical constructions) all their own.

We are going to react with faint but tolerant amusement at these good souls with their fustian accents, self-made syntax, and homespun humour. But we shall work hard and do our bit and learn the lingo, and in no time at all we shall be fully integrated into this quaint society with a completely different sense of time and a different philosophy of the world, both of which we shall embrace and adopt as we grow to appreciate a New View of Life.

If one had to sum it up in a single sentence, we look forward to hearing (and – who knows? – speaking) a paradisal patois epitomised (wrongly) by the BBC Drama Department – Rural English Accent on a bad day.

What actually happened, of course, was that the preconceptions were splintered into so many pieces that one hardly knows which one to pick up to give an impression of the truth. Not that the truth was painful – just, generally, surprising.

Well, all right, here goes.

For a start, there isn't a Devon accent. Not one. There are several – maybe many, for all I know; though constant travel, the resultant integration, and the media, are ironing these differences out.

The minute you stop to think about it, it's common sense. London has more than one accent (and London is much smaller than Devon); not everyone talks like a Cockney. My goodness, think of all the immigrant communities. And, immigrants or no immigrants, people of Kent on one side of London don't talk like people of Essex on the other.

Professor Henry Higgins in Shaw's *Pygmalion* claimed that he was such an accurate observer of people's pronunciation habits that he could place a man within a few miles in London, sometimes within a few streets. He guessed, with disturbing correctness, that Eliza came from Lisson Grove. Eliza was predictably, and understandably, stunned.

I am not an authority on phonetics or philology, or, I hope, a bombast like Henry Higgins (curious that Shaw gave him such a commonplace, non-academic surname; perhaps he was just making an ironic joke all of his own), so I can lay no claim to such expertise. But I did catch on to the fact that not all Devonians spoke the same – town areas and rural areas, North Devon and South Devon, for instance. Even by age. Our modern education system, and the BBC, inevitably induce a degree of uniformity, and children tend to emulate the noises around them. But once they leave school, and join adult life, it is different. If they stay in Devon – and a lot do – they tend slowly to revert. So the accents (or lack of them) that you hear in a Barnstaple comprehensive school can be somewhat distant from the retro badinage between middle-aged stallholders in Barnstaple Pannier Market.

It's contact, or the lack of it. I once taught a boy who lived on a remote farm (which was nevertheless only five or ten miles from Barnstaple). All he saw of life during the week was the school bus and the classroom. His mother, who didn't drive, saw even less. She was lucky if she got away from the premises in the family Land

Rover once a week. So the only people this family spoke to, by and large, were themselves. Because they knew each other so well, words became less and less necessary. So this lad – let us call him Peter – was simply not in the habit of speaking much, if at all, for hours at a time. If I asked him a simple question, for instance, the answer 'Yes' became a minute tilt of the chin.

But of course, when he *did* speak, Peter had an accent.

That was not the full extent of it. We discovered shortly after moving in that we had a 'neighbour' (in a community like Devon, the third or fourth biggest county, distance was relative) – we had a neighbour who had been raised on a farm right out in the middle of Exmoor. Miles from anywhere. I would venture to guess, from what I found out about him, that he had not been the world's best attender at school. So he saw even less of the world.

I've said this already, but please excuse the repetition; it is so relevant and apt.

David had an accent all right. For six months I couldn't understand a thing he said. He had married a girl from London or Essex (I forget which); it must have been a major culture shock for both of them. With such linguistic barriers between them, the animal magnetism between them must have been of a very high voltage to help them sustain the first year or two of marriage.

To us 'Grockles', David (another David) was impenetrable. Not wary, not stand-offish, not unkind, not unhelpful, not negative in any way – just impenetrable.

However, most of the Devonians we spoke to were pretty normal. A Devon 'tang' naturally, but quite easy to follow. Some slightly unexpectedly literary adjectives crept into the conversation – 'abusive' is one I remember. This from a gritty elderly farmer in tweeds, knee-length leather gaiters, and immovable flat cap.

Some engaging phrases threw dashes of welcome spice into the proceedings, like curry into a stew. When asked why he suffered so much from chronic back pain, a wiry builder said to us with totally prompt honesty, 'Yurrs of aboose.'

Another, rather endearing, epithet was/is their way of referring to a young daughter – 'my little maid'. Little idiomatic forms of address appeared regularly: 'My dere' is an obvious one, offered, with no edge, to either sex, and between men sometimes. Better still, the lady who gave you your change for the purchase of home-made marmalade in the Pannier Market would say, 'There y'are, my lover', with a gentle, lingering roll on the final 'r'.

Perhaps the 'Devon accent' (although I said it didn't exist) was lurking under the surface all the time. Several years later we had a butcher who, if he was so inclined, could lay it on thick, and sound like my early Exmoor neighbour. I have sat in a Devon audience and laughed with everybody else at recitations in the 'Devon accent' – eons away from BBC Rural. Very rich, and very subtle, but not common, I venture to remark, not these days. Anyway, it seems that many of them can put it on when they want to.

But, as I said earlier, we never caught any of it. (So much for the mellifluous linguistic integration that the dreamers look forward to.) Just a little of this Devonian shine, you would have thought, might have rubbed off on us. Not on my wife and me, of course; we were too far gone. We had 'South-East' written all over us, and remained that way. But you might have expected that our three boys would have absorbed something.

Not so. Stepsons Christopher (8) and Martin (6) remained steadfastly Thames Ditton. Our new arrival Stephen (born in 1972) proved to be permeable enough to be able, later, to *put on* a Devon accent, but his normal speech is South-East too. Listening to him, you would never guess that he was raised in Devon.

Quite what that proves I don't know – if it proves anything. But I thought it might put a few cards on the table.

*

When I began teaching at Barnstaple Grammar School (as it then was – it went comprehensive in 1972), I took mostly History; it was my degree subject. But I collected a few English classes too.

As you know, English teaching involves getting pupils to express

162

themselves on paper – 'essays', 'composition', writing, whatever you care to call it. It is not easy to devise topics on which pupils can create connected prose. The vast majority of children are not creative writers. The challenge is to think of something which will fire their interest or imagination, or at least their willingness to have a go. Preferably something on which they genuinely feel they may have something to say, not what they think their teachers want them to say.

It was here that the Devon accent, like the US cavalry, came galloping to the rescue. I discovered Arthur J. Coles.

In the early decades of the twentieth century, Arthur Coles, who was presumably Devon-born, wrote a regular piece in the *Devon and Exeter Gazette* – in the Devon accent. In an inspired moment he chose to write under the pen name of 'Jan Stewer'. It encapsulated with poetic perfection Devon and the Devonian – his parochialism, shrewdness, humour, and fondness for gossip and a good story.

(Here I face a problem regularly confessed to by P.G. Wodehouse: how much do you explain and how much do you assume the reader already knows and understands? In PGW's case, how much does the reader of the newest Bertie Wooster story know about the earlier episodes in his biography – his many escapades in country houses late at night, or his many narrow escapes from the marital clutches of the likes of Cora Bellinger, Madeline Bassett, Bobby Wickham, and others. How much are they going to feel frustrated at being denied the background, or how much are they going to feel miffed at having their intelligence, or at least their memory, insulted?)

So forgive me if I insert here the titbit of background to the effect that Jan Stewer was one of the men who accompanied Bill Brewer, Peter Gurney, Peter Davy, Dan'l Whiddon, 'Arry 'Awk, and Uncle Tom Cobbleigh on Tom Pearce's grey mare to Widdicombe Fair. Should I even, in these days of the ubiquity of pop music (to the exclusion of much else), explain that *Widdicombe Fair* was a popular and much-sung song in past years? And that Widdicombe is a real place, and where it is? For many readers, in the post-war pop world of Elvis, Cliff, the Punks, the Rolling Floyd, the Pink Oasis, and Sex Grunge Metal, Widdicombe and its fair may have simply slipped off the flat earth of folk music.

Anyway, Arthur Coles wrote in the Devon accent. How do you put on paper a sound? An accent? Two ways mostly – by means of using local idiom, and secondly by the phonetic use of spelling. So 'we laughed out loud' became 'didn' us laaf'. 'You silly fool' emerged as 'Thee gurt stoobid'. And so on. It was all beautifully observed.

I fell on this. I like reading out loud. Children of all ages and stages like being read to. And it was perfect ammunition for a homework essay afterwards. Something like: 'Tell the story of a famous nursery tale in the Devon accent.' And you use Jan Stewer to give examples of what you want.

I did my best to attempt a Devon accent. It would probably have caused grimaces of pain to appear on the face of an expert reciter, but I could get away with it – just – in the classroom. Incidentally, I found that some of the words Coles used were unknown even to modern Devon adults. When I asked someone whether he knew what 'jewsive' meant, he said he didn't know. (According to Jan, if someone had 'bad teeths-ache', it hurt 'most jewsive'.) 'Tantaddlin' baskit' is another relic now not used (well, not in my hearing), though perhaps one could hazard a guess at its meaning.

I was surprised to discover that much of it offered the entertainment of novelty to a lot of classes. Not that they had never heard the Devon accent; of course they had. They lived with it all around them, insofar as I have indicated above. But many of them were second- and third-generation housing estate, reared not on marbles and conkers but on the box. (Nowadays of course we are way beyond the box; it's a whole new Trinity: Google the Father, Text the Son, and Twitter the Holy Ghost.)

It would appear that a lot of rural instinct has gone, though some habits are still there. The name is not 'Sharon' but 'Sharin'. You don't go 'to' Barnstaple; you go 'down' Barnstaple. You even go 'down' London. 'Are you going to the tutor group?' becomes 'be you gwain done tud'r?' It's the little words. And why do they change, as sometimes they do? Not long ago, if it was your responsibility, it was 'up to you'. Now it is 'down to you'. Why?

Be all that as it may, my point is that many of these children found the spoken Devon accent amusing – even mine (though maybe for different reasons). So when I set the English homework, just as I had fallen on Arthur J. Coles, they fell on him too. After all, how often did the chance come along in a homework to spell words 'wrong', on purpose, and get them marked 'right'?

Thanks to Jan Stewer, I often got some of the best homeworks of the year.

*

I would warm them up first with an exercise to demonstrate the vagaries of English spelling. Tell a short story, relate an event, even give the weather forecast – with total phonetic accuracy, rendering the words exactly as they are pronounced. 'Knsider haow werds akshully saound.'

And they did. Like Holmes, they actually observed. I kept some of the best ones. How about these?

Opisit sooige (awful stuff) cumphtabul Barklees (the bank) elifant (aka Nellie) warlls (which have ears)

Or, more involved:

Fyuw (well, not many) scjesstid (what a good idea) skwair (not circular) coodant (impossible)

And work these out:

N e one n-counter r'vuw

Some showed almost laser-like accuracy:

Aneesirtist petrifiid (note the third 'i') yoozhooallee syd erfect

Some lovely sentences stuck in the mind:

'Mirra, mirra, on the wawl'; 'the wich stawmed in, a wurlwind of fewery'; 'hoo's bin eeting mi porrij?'

And, if I didn't append the translation, how many of you would have worked out what 'Yrnetn' meant? Look it up at the end of the chapter.

So they were pretty well primed with what was wanted by the

time I set an essay-story in the Devon accent. I got a lot of really good stuff, some of which was sustained for two or three pages. I can't put in whole pieces; it would be too much of a good thing. But I would ask you to give this final offering a go: it is a small set of excerpts from the story of Rumpelstiltskin.

'There were wonse a miller, 'oo were pawer, boot 'e 'ad a boodiful dawter. Won day 'e 'ad 'oo spake to de Keng, and, to gain empordence, de stupaird miller said to 'im, "Oi 'ave a dawter 'oo can spen strawer en'o gauld . . ."'

'The gerl were b'ought 'o the Keng the nex' day and 'e led 'er en'o a rumeful o' strawer. 'E give 'er a spenning whell and saird, "Now get down 'oo work at wonse. And if ee 'aven't spun this 'ere strawer en'o gauld boi the mawnen, ee shull doi!" Then 'ee locked the rume, and lef' the gerl awl alown.'

'The gerl beganoo to croi, but soudenly the dawer flew aupen, a toinee lettal man com en and saired, "Gud evenin', woi yew be croien soo bitterlay?" '

[As you know, the dwarf span the gold for her. He demanded payment, and she gave him all she had. It was not enough. Luckily, she found favour with the King (all that gold), married him, and had a child, but the dwarf had gone and spoilt it by demanding the baby as payment unless she could guess his name. Now read on:]

'The Queen [well, she was now] thawt awl noight long o' all 'e nairms shay 'ad ever 'erd. When the lettal man appeared the followen day, she. . . gave awl the nairms shay knew wan after nuther. But 'oo evry wan'o them the lettal man saird, "T'ain't moi nairm." '

[Don't miss the next thrilling instalment.]

All right, so the cynics among you could suspect that there may well have been a spot of assistance from the old folks at home. But the *concept* must reflect credit on the pupil, *and* the industry. It also demonstrates great co-operation and willingness.

Timely help or not, it's good, isn't it? And so well sustained. I typed it out to keep it; it came to two solid pages of A4. I loved the 'woi yew be croien soo bitterlay?' Spot on.

*

So how many questions have I answered about Devon and its accents? Probably very few, if any. Is 'Devonian' at the folk song and relic stage? Is it alive and well? Is it developing? Has the study of Devonian got a grant from the European Community? (Well, it won't now, will it?) Is there a single school where Devonian is encouraged? (You know, like Welsh or Erse.)

My reply has to be, in effect, 'I have no idea.' All I have done is to give you a whistle-stop tour of some of the counters where Devonian is on offer. Your conclusions will be like impressions from glances in shop windows.

The best I can hope for is to have convinced you that 'Devonian' (with the inverted commas this time), is most certainly there, and it is rich, and (whatever it is) it is worth keeping.

If you want to find out more, you can always come and see, or rather hear, for yourself, can't you? ' 'Tis truh, mah dere, 'Tis truh.'

Oh, yes – 'yrnetn'. Wire netting.

18

Raising

Most gardens grow vegetables; we grew boys. Three. For five years. Two of them, Christopher and Martin, came to it at eight and six years respectively; Stephen was born there. How did they grow? Was it good ground for them? Like plants, did they 'take'? How deep were the roots they put down?

What were the chances? What were the prospects? What were the beckonings? What were the warnings?

After the previous seventeen chapters, I hope it has become clear that New Mill was, at the very least, a bit unusual. There was no means by which it could be run, or described, as an ordinary suburban semi, or any other kind of semi. It didn't look like a semi; no pebble-dash, no mock Tudor beams on the front façade, no tidy right angles everywhere, no car-port, no garage. Nor did it look like an old house tarted up to look modern – you know, huge window panes, solar panels, poly-this and poly-that. There was no front garden, and no back garden – just a sort of all-around garden, which uncharitably-disposed observers would have described as an apology for a field. No post-box just up the road. No road. So no kerb, no drains, no gutters. No street lamps, because there was no street. No houses next door. One could go on – no central heating, no double-glazing, no cavity-wall insulation (it was just one bloody great thick stone wall). And inside – well, it was little short of a depressed area, by today's standards. No television, no phone, no microwave, no dishwasher, no fitted carpets, no mains gas, no mains drainage, no computer (obviously – this was the early 1970's). If you tried to bring up a family in a house like this

168

today, you would stand a good chance of being visited by various agencies of 'welfare'.

As if that were not enough, outside the place bristled with risks and hazards – steep gradients, jutting stones, brambles, nettles, rickety fences, barbed wire, a looming sycamore (which, if a storm had been bad enough, could have fallen and demolished half the building), and of course the river. All right, it was called only 'Ilkerton Water' on the Ordnance Survey map, but it was a 'water' which had nearly carried away *the whole building* in 1952. To repeat, we began with two boys aged six and eight, and just over a year later we had a new-born infant. So again the health and safety brigade would have had a fit.

Put like that, it sounds like the archetypal Shocking Example – a melange of Cold Comfort Farm, Dotheboys Hall, and the Château d'If. Dear God! What were we doing there?

But it was never put like that – well, not to us, not at the time. It all depends on which evidence you select to build your picture. If you said of a certain historical figure that he was a failure at school; that he was undersized; that he had a speech impediment; that he scraped his way into the Army because his parents could not get him in anywhere else; that he left a few years later because he could not afford the life of a cavalry officer; that he was captured in a war; that he was sacked from the Government because he was blamed for one of the major disasters of the war; that he spent years in opposition, with nobody listening to him; that after a serious road accident, he was written off; and that he died after most of his faculties had faded – if you said all that, and nothing else, one would never guess you were writing about Winston Churchill. Every single item in that summary is true, but of course it does not begin to approach the whole truth.

We were aware of all the things I have described, obviously, but we did not think of all of them at the same time. There were too many other things to think about. We just did the *next* thing.

So did the boys. Considering that Christopher and Martin were the products of suburban semi's, and had never before spent time in a place remotely like New Mill, they adapted pretty well, I thought. Stephen was born to it, so it was easier for him; he had never known anything else. And he had two older brothers to keep an eye on him, to shield him, to watch out for him. It was an advantage that there was an age gap between them. In second marriages, there is always the risk of what the psychologists call 'sibling rivalry'. Not so with us: the age gap (nearly eight and ten years by the time he was born) meant that they never saw him as a rival. He was an interesting 'extra', a perfect fall guy for exploits, a mascot. On his side, he saw Christopher and Martin as brothers, never as step-brothers. And so have they remained.

New Mill, and North Devon as a whole, was a great presenter of challenges, problems, and novelties to two boys with the background I have set out, so, if nothing else, it was absorbing. Their own personalities, even at six and eight, were well enough formed to be able to give them the wherewithal to deal with whatever they met.

School, for example. A new school is a new school, in Surrey or Devon. Christopher was clearly bright, he was a conformist, and he was diligent, so he would have succeeded regardless. He did the work, he took no risks, and he made good progress. He made friends with a boy who is his friend to this day. It was the same when he moved on to Ilfracombe Comprehensive. When we left New Mill, and he had to move to the comprehensive school at Barnstaple (having changed its name from 'Barnstaple Grammar School' to the 'Park' school), he did exactly the same there. After that, he worked hard in the sixth form of a public school. He worked hard at university, and he has worked hard ever since, and has a great deal to show for it (all well deserved). So New Mill, in that sense, was almost incidental. His character and personality were such that he would have done well anywhere.

So too with Martin, though in a more indirect way. At six you wouldn't have held out the same hopes for him as you did with Christopher. A slight tongue-tie meant that he did not always speak clearly. He was left-handed. He was probably slightly overshadowed by Christopher, who was already cast as the 'successful' brother of the two. He was backward with reading, never gaining any real fluency till he was eight or nine.

The Lynton headmaster, Harold Jester, however, told us, more than once, that we had nothing to worry about with Martin. Like all good schoolmasters, he could see through the snags and obstacles and disadvantages; he could see that all the marbles were there, and in the right order. Martin, on his side, knew what he knew; he did not concern himself with the worries of those about him. He worked at his own pace and in his own way. As long as life provided a sufficient supply of sums, wires, and Lego, he was perfectly content. And, as with Christopher, he has prospered; he now designs computer programmes, very profitably. As with Christopher once more, school was to a large extent incidental.

So much for school. They approached and dealt with New Mill in the same way. They brought their individual talents and interests to bear; they did not bemoan the absence of suburban comforts and advantages (well, they didn't to me); and they took advantage of the opportunities that opened before them. The natural curiosity and energy of youth did the rest.

For a start, there was nothing formal about New Mill. We were not churchgoers, so there was no need of 'best clothes for Sunday'. They dressed well for school, but after that it was tee-shirts, jeans, jumpers, and boats. Boats? I discovered (not original really; I simply tumbled to what thousands of other parents had tumbled to) that one could buy lightweight blue canvas, slip-on footwear that did for everything. We did not insist on slippers indoors. I don't think either of them ever possessed a pair of slippers. We did not insist on shoes coming off the minute they walked in the front door. It was simply not that sort of house. We had no expensive carpets to spoil, and no polished floors.

I don't know how the word 'boats' evolved. Again, I don't suppose it was original. But it fitted. The boats, like the word, fitted easily; they were easy to put on and slide off; they could be easily washed and dried; if they broke down at the back, they were still wearable, like ex-pats' espadrilles; they took a deal of punishment; they were easily replaced; and they were cheap. They never set out to be smart, so they had immediate and automatic appeal to boys out of school. Boats went into New Mill vernacular, along with the fuchsials, the japonical, and the occasional bout of diarrhoeal.

Tee-shirts, jumpers and jeans performed similarly. Missing buttons, baggy waists, saggy sleeves, dangling threads, holes, stains simply did not matter. We had few gadgets, true, but we did have a washing machine, so there was no danger of ghastly outbreaks of epidemic disease. There were no neighbours to pass remarks, no Joneses to keep up with.

Jeans were indestructible; they stood up to anything that New Mill could dish out. They seemed vulnerable only to water. And that was to prove Martin's nemesis.

There is something about running water. Rivers and streams are beguiling, evocative, irresistible, almost hypnotic. Think of the first impact of the river on Mole in *The Wind in the Willows*. Think of Tennyson's brook; think of Old Man River; think of Schubert's trout; think of Old Father Thames. Think of Ratty's love of the river: 'By it and with it and on it and in it. . . It's brother and sister to me, and aunts, and company, and food and drink, and (naturally) washing.'

Mole had never lived near running water, so he was going to be bowled over by 'this sleek, sinuous, full-bodied animal'. I think the river hit Christopher and Martin in a similar way. It was bound to; they had lived in a suburban semi. all their lives. The very name of Mole's house – 'Mole End' – somehow signified something sheltered, unworldly, innocent. Before New Mill, the two boys had lived in a road called 'Endway'.

Like Mole, they took to the river. They discovered, in their school holidays and weekends, that, as Ratty said, 'There is *nothing* – absolutely nothing – half so much worth doing as simply messing about in boats.' For 'boats' read 'streams'.

I have no idea about the full extent of what they got up to – probably just as well – but I do know that they derived a great of pleasure and contentment from simply, as Ratty said, 'messing about'.

It is possible that Martin got just a little bit more out of it than Christopher did, but there was not much in it. Though there were one or two happenings that might well have dampened his enthusiasm, in more than one sense of the word.

The first episode to work its way into family folklore came when Martin was engaged in some business or other on the edge of the stream. We were not there; we were sitting outside the house, on the little patch of grass which I had tamed sufficiently to enable us to take genteel tea out of doors.

The first thing we saw was Martin walking purposefully towards us, dripping all over the place. He had managed to fall in – slipped down a bank, fallen off a boulder, overbalanced from the narrow bridge. We didn't ask because he was clearly on his determined way to the bedroom to change his clothes.

Off he went, back to the stream, and we turned back to our tea and buns. A short while later back he came again, in the same condition as before. The brow was lower, and he was in even less mood to offer explanations. In the house, up the stairs, fresh set of frowsy jumpers and frayed jeans

Back to the stream for him, and back to the strawberry jam for us.

I don't remember how long afterwards it was, but it wasn't long, we do know that. Martin was bent over with mortification. He didn't walk; he stumped. We did not dare to ask questions, because his condition was blindingly obvious. In any case, he was totally beyond words. He marched into the house yet again, went straight upstairs, took off his clothes for the third time – and put himself to bed.

The second event to be transmogrified into legend was the business of Christopher's boat. A real boat this time, not his left shoe.

Christopher had made a boat – out of the usual mish-mash of bits of old wood, rusty nails, any old iron he found about the place (Ken's workshop was an Aladdin's cave for this sort of thing), and the ubiquitous binder twine. Near the end of the property there was a smooth stretch of water relatively free from large rocks and overhanging foliage. Half-way along it was crossed by a slender bridge manufactured out of iron and concrete. Don't ask me how they built a bridge with concrete over a stream out on the edge of Exmoor. Just take it from me that there was a thin bridge over the stream, only about eighteen inches wide, and it was made of concrete. I think a couple of iron stanchions were placed on either side to offer minimal support for the not-so-intrepid, but that was about it.

It didn't put Martin off. He had recovered, or forgotten about, his triple inundation, and there he was, barelegged and barefoot, in the middle of the bridge. Why? Because Christopher had launched his boat a few yards above the bridge, and was about to sail it underneath. No prizes for guessing what Martin had in mind. Any doubt would have been removed by the sight of the hefty stone he clutched. I say 'hefty' because he needed both hands to hold it.

He stood on the lower side of the bridge, bending over slightly in anticipation, and poising the bomb until the *Titanic* should appear between his feet. To stabilise himself, he had hooked his toes round the edge of the concrete.

Well, it was 'bombs gone' all right. The only trouble was that he did not hit the *Titanic*; he dropped – nay, *threw* – the stone straight on to his bare foot. The pain must have been indescribable. It was a miracle that nothing was broken. Certainly not the boat.

Despite the mishaps I have mentioned, and no doubt others which I still know nothing about, it is interesting that Martin now has a permanently running water feature in his garden.

*

Christopher had the good sense, or the good luck, not to fall in, but he must have got a bit wet now and then. He and Martin discovered an old tin bath – the sort that miners were supposed to have used in front of their parlour fire on a Saturday night. New Mill was the sort of place where you found things like that.

When you have a vessel the size of a boat, and running water nearby, it's pretty obvious what you're going to do with it. Or at least try to do with it. They dragged it to the stream, in an unconscious, if puny, imitation of the lugging of the Lynmouth lifeboat over Countisbury Hill. They succeeded in launching it, though spoil-sport parents did not provide any bottle of champers to mark the occasion. As with so many other things they got up to, I don't think we had any idea. They went on board.

There was only one snag: there was a hole in the bottom. Martin still maintains that they got a bit of mileage out of it. It depends of course on the size of the hole, but the whole incident reeks of New Mill.

Then there was the episode of the Lambretta. James, one of the two brothers who lived up the valley in the stables and guest house, found a broken-down motor scooter. As I have just said, you don't ask questions about things like that; you just accept them. James found a Lambretta? Well, OK. If he had stumbled across the remains of a shot-down Messerschmitt, I think we would have accepted that too as unremarkable.

At any rate, James set himself the task of putting it back into commission. Christopher found himself roped into that. James had access to all sorts of tools, benches, and gadgets at his house, and he had an above average mechanical instinct. And he was a year or two older than Christopher. Big lad too.

Believe it or not, they got it going. James rode it round the field. So did Christopher. Both were under age. But this was Devon, and this was New Mill. You did that sort of thing.

Christopher discovered fishing. James probably put him up to that too. He was quite successful. I won't say we fed regularly on fresh fish, but, memorably, he once provided freshly-caught trout for a dinner party; our guests talked about it for months afterwards.

James' younger brother Andrew was often one of the party. Almost exactly Christopher's age. Not as mechanical as James, not as ingenious perhaps, but he had his contribution to make. He was undemanding, but good company. He had such a quiet, settled, contemplative face that he could have passed for a philosopher or a saint. When Mrs. Coates once caught sight of him between a couple of lambs, she said he reminded her of Jesus.

All four of them got on well; there were no jarring incidents that I recall. This is partly attributable of course to their easy-going natures, but it may also be explained by the fact that there were always so many absorbing things to do. So much disagreement among boys (and girls too, I should guess) comes about from boredom. You can't say that anything *happened* at New Mill, any more than you say that anything much has happened in Devon since the Norman Conquest. It was just that there always seemed to be something to do, and worth doing.

Back to the Water Rat again: 'You're always busy, and you never do anything in particular; and when you've done it, there's always something else to do, and you can do it if you like.'

Both we and James and Andrew's parents gave them the run of both establishments, and they came and went whenever they felt like it, and nobody minded. Nobody ever told them to bring their slippers with them.

Andrew once accompanied us to a village called Bradworthy to buy some furniture. I don't know how it came about, but there he was in the back of the Land Rover, with Christopher and Martin, and Stephen strapped in somewhere. It may have been the old Land Rover, so it was a minor miracle that we got there – and back – without a single door falling off.

We had heard that there was this artisan who made very good pine furniture, and very reasonably. So off we went. He had a very odd name – Piplak. It turned out that he was German. He had been taken prisoner in the War, and had ended up in a prison camp in England. For reasons we never discovered, he stayed on here when the War was over, and set himself up as a carpenter and joiner. Perhaps the fact that he married an English girl called Eve went a long way to explain it.

He clearly knew his business. He sold us a kitchen table which we still have, and it has matured into a much-respected piece of furniture, well worn and full of character. Mr. Piplak made furniture to last. As he put it, it was all 'very shtrong.' There was still a great deal of Central Europe running through his speech.

The table was in pieces, and we were to assemble it when we got home. It was easy too; even I was able to do it. It was quite a ride back – Mr. and Mrs. Coates up front; Stephen somewhere which I forget, and three boys among the disassembled portions of a new pine table, all in one Land Rover. And it all cost £17. (The table, not the Land Rover.)

We also bought four stools – a mere £4.00 each. We still have those too – 'very shtrong', you see. Some time later, we bought a Welsh dresser – shelves, cupboards, black iron hinges and handles – £36.00. We have had it for forty years, and the doors still shut like silk.

Christopher has reminded me of things I had forgotten. The spanner we had to use to flush the toilet in the very early days. The resident bat in Ken's workshop. Martin added the beam above the deserted mill section that was struck by lightning. I myself remember Martin spending almost the whole day using mud to re-point and render an entire wall of the disused outside toilet at the end of the building.

'. . . . when you've done it, there's always something else to do, and you can do it if you like. . . '

Well, Martin did like. He got plastered with mud from head to foot. But it seemed such a good idea at the time.

19

Reaching Out

The bus could take you to Lynton one way and Barnstaple the other, and, if you didn't mind changing at the bus station, to Exeter and beyond, even to London if you were so disposed. In fact, if you had the time, a good book, and a sandwich or two, you could go pretty well anywhere.

If you had sound footwear, wind, and limb, there was a great deal to see nearer home, at a much slower pace, as I described in Chapter Eight.

But that was not the half of it. Devon is a big county, the fourth biggest in the land. Yorkshire you would expect to be the biggest, and it is. North Yorkshire actually. The other chunks are smaller, but imagine the imbalance if you combined them, as one did years ago. All those Ridings.

Similarly, you would not be surprised to discover that the second biggest is Lincolnshire. But the surprise comes with the third biggest – Cumbria. How many of you knew that? All right, so it is only 60 square kilometres bigger than Devon, but I bet the Cumbrians regard those sixty as quite important. Anything to put Devonians in their place.

What I am getting at in a roundabout way, and what I am sure you have already divined, is the importance in a county like Devon of the internal combustion engine – the motor car. Or, in our case, the Land Rover, both the old one and the new one. Same vehicle basically, same seating capacity (well, ours were), and similar performance, though of course not the same in reliability. The new one had its off moments, but at least it could be relied upon not to shed doors on the Queen's highway.

To be honest, it was not all that much more comfortable. Fewer draughts, maybe. But apart from the seats, there was a distinct shortage of upholstery, and an awful lot of bare metal. The only aid to comfort was a heater that took an unconscionable time to kick in. There were so many edges and sharp corners in the back that I had a metal bar put in round the spare wheel that the boys could hang on to. Conversation inside was inclined to be intermittent because of a vociferous engine. It was no sprinter from a standing start, and I never had the nerve to drive it (the new one) much more than seventy miles an hour. So – no rally tiger. (The idea of driving the old one at seventy was made in dreamland.)

It wasn't all bad. A Land Rover was a Land Rover – a name to conjure with. Just as nobody does wine like the French, and nobody used to do vacuum cleaners like Hoover's, so nobody does tough 4 x 4's quite like Land Rover. It had a fittingly rustic colour – we didn't go for any exotic tints; 'Land Rover Green' suited us fine. It fitted the countryside. Indeed, it fitted everything. A Land Rover was, and is, the sort of vehicle you could take anywhere and not be out of place – town markets, county shows (obviously), plush weddings, posh hotels, even stately homes. You could get out of it wearing overalls, jeans, plus fours, a DJ – anything. And not only in the 'country'. I once parked just off Trafalgar Square, and nobody nudged his neighbour to point, or smiled and shook his head. Indeed, on roads like the North Circular, saloon car drivers treated me with noticeable respect. In other words, it was rugged, and every man likes to own something rugged.

That was not the end of it. It was very roomy. It was ideal for large items like new tables bought from carpenters in Bradworthy. You could put newly-filled paraffin drums or fresh gas cylinders in the back without worrying about staining the leather seats, because there weren't any. With three boys to consider, and, later, a load of camping equipment, you needed a lot of space.

I now own a Freelander, which has many virtues, but lofty space is not one of them. I could drive the Land Rover with a trilby hat on (which shows you how long ago this was). In the Freelander it's a squeeze to get your head in, never mind a hat.

Perhaps most relevant to our situation, it could handle bends, steep hills, and poor surfaces. That was what it had been designed to do. So it could deal with New Mill Lane with one hand tied behind its back. What a luxury to be able to drive it all the way down and park it in the broken old 'mill' end of the house and thence only ten yards on foot to the lounge. (No porch or hall; you opened the front door and you were in.)

So, we travelled.

We started in a small way. The nearest village on the way to Barnstaple was Parracombe. It was in a deep valley. The road therefore, from either direction, was 1 in 4. Shortly before we came to live there, they built a road right round it, called, I believe, somewhat grandiloquently, the 'Parracombe By-Pass'. You half expected to encounter young bloods in blazers and cheesecutter caps out for a spin with their girl friends in the Aston or the Bugatti. The reality was more likely to be an enormous, rumbling muck-spreader behind an even muddier tractor, proceeding at a much more sedate pace, like butlers in P.G. Wodehouse novels.

Many Devonians still used the old road, partly I suspect from cussed habit, and partly because the journey was much shorter, and, when we were feeling adventurous and the roads were not icy, we did too. If you did begin to slide on the ice on a 1 in 4 gradient, you were unlikely to stop before you hit the bottom outside the *Fox and Grapes,* and that was only because of the rising gradient on the other side.

Devon was a stern mentor to those who were used to top gear and very little else, like our cheesecutter cap young man in his drop-head coupé. The gradients I have already referred to. There were so many hills that, perforce, at any rate if you wished to survive, you learned to cope with them. Tourists who complained about them would draw knowing smiles from us natives and veterans. We knew them all – Lynmouth, Countisbsury, Porlock, Parracombe, the old Lynton coach road. There was one village called Charles that boasted a gradient of 1 in 3. Well, that's what they used to say.

I have already referred to the shattered lorry driver who had just arrived in Lynton from South Wales. He was delivering a load to the coal yard behind the bus station. I can't reproduce his accent in print, but take it from me the trauma of the journey over Porlock, Countisbury and Lynmouth had enriched his Welshness no end. Almost what you might call a Broken Man.

That was not the end of it. Bends were sharper, and could go on for what seemed more than the possible 360 degrees. Devon is notorious for its very high hedges and hedge-banks, so that too could spring a lot of surprises. Tractors could edge out of hidden field gates. Flocks of sheep could spring at you from sudden turns, like the Demon King in pantomime.

You learned respect.

Before we leave Parracombe, I should like to put on record one of the saddest sights we ever saw in our time at New Mill.

It rains quite a lot in Devon. The high ground, you see – Exmoor and Dartmoor. To say nothing of the proximity of western rain-bearing winds from the Bristol Channel and the Atlantic. Think of the geography lessons you should have paid more attention to at school. And there is the very old story, about the view from the North Devon coast towards South Wales (and I'm sure it is told about dozens of views all over England). 'If you can see the South Wales coast clearly, it means it is going to rain; if you can't see it, it already is raining.'

Well, we were driving through Parracombe (on our way to Barnstaple presumably). We had chosen to give the by-pass a miss and went down the old road. It was the Whitsun weekend, and we had heard that there were going to be some junketings in the village to mark the Bank Holiday.

It was raining, of course. And not just gentle drizzle; this was the real McCoy – a steady downpour that reeked of permanence. As we descended, we noticed that there was nobody about. We saw no sign of 'junketings', or any sign of preparation for 'junketings'. Everything was grey and drooping.

The further we went down, the gloomier and more desolate it looked. At last we got to the bottom, by the *Fox and Grapes*. There, strung across the road, was a solitary line of bunting, every piece of which was practically running with water. In the middle of the bunting was another banner, on which was printed 'Parracombe Revels'.

It made you think of all the committee meetings and preparations and letters written and permits sought and lorries hired and willing ladies making cakes and local tradesmen contributing produce – all for that dripping bunting – the Parracombe Revels. It would have been bearable if it had been 'the Parracombe Show' or 'Parracombe Village Fete'. But 'Revels'. It conveyed the Middle Ages, maypoles, miracle plays, and, thrown in for good measure, a tinsel-trimmed jester and a guest appearance by the Pied Piper of Hamelin.

There was nobody there. I repeat, it was one of the saddest sights.

We used the Land Rover, naturally, to see the sights Devon has to offer, the ones which appear in all the brochures. We wandered all over the Valley of the Rocks just outside Lynton, and speculated about the goats that are said to roam at will. We walked right down the interminable main street that is about all there is of Combe Martin. Well, that is how it struck us; perhaps we did not try hard enough. I came across a telling little piece of information to illustrate how the language changes. 'Combe Martin' is written as two words. In my present work as a school archivist, I saw in one of the school magazines from a century ago the spelling 'Combmartin'. Similarly, I found the rendering of the game where you propelled the ball with the foot as, logically, 'foot ball'. Two words. A few decades later, the magazines used to print 'foot-ball'. Finally, of course, came 'football'. Now why? What are the mechanics of this? Laziness? Ignorance? Fashion?

In this section of North Devon you can find what they say is the smallest parish church in England – at Culbone. It is off the main road – of course. You have to park at the side of a path, and walk a fair step to reach the church. And my word, it is small. The nave is less than 22 feet long, and the whole church is only 35. It can seat 30 people. It would be interesting to know how many services they have there in a year.

But it is far from negligible. It has a venerable ancestry, maybe even pre-Norman. It is mentioned in Domesday Book. Its saint is St Beuno. No – neither had I. Welsh, apparently. Devon is full of old things like this. Going back to Parracombe for a minute, as you descend the old road and look down on the land around the village, you can see the remains of the old motte-and-bailey castle built by the new Norman occupiers. That's one thing about Devon: it is so old and its landscape is so definite, well hewn, and clear-cut that there is often only one possible place you could have put the settlements, and of course they are still there, for the same reasons. I should guess that Devon has more than its share of Saxon place-names.

Culbone looks neat and tidy too. The photograph provided by our regular informant, Mr. Google, and by all the guide brochures, shows a building that sits easily on the eye. Forty or so years ago, I got the bug for painting. One day I was laid up with some cold virus or other, and, for want of anything better to do, I had a crack at a water-colour of Culbone. Beginner's luck, maybe, but it didn't come out too badly. At any rate, I was taken enough by my own work to have it framed, and I have it still. Its presence on the wall is assured by sentiment rather than by merit, but it has a firm place in the Coates household nonetheless.

Over the five years we were there, we did many of the usual touristy things. Well, you would, wouldn't you? They were there.

We made the acquaintance of Simonsbath. (Remember? Not 'Seyemonsbath' but 'Simmonsbath'.) One of the Knight creations from the nineteenth century. Way out, smack in the middle of the Moor. Talk about remote.

Exmoor may be only thirty-odd miles across, but it is also officially a wilderness, with good reason. Try Exehead or The Chains if you don't believe me. You could die of exposure on Exmoor if you were stupid enough. I have already mentioned the bent-over hedges and the bogs. (Think of Farmer Mole, and no doubt other cocky, overfilled travellers on wild nights). The lack of trees too. The hardy sheep, so tough and independent that they take no notice whatever of motor vehicles as they graze the grass verges of the roads.

Nobody farms now right out on the Moor. Well, not in the Knight-founded farms. Not with the primitive facilities available to the men of the nineteenth century. When they have tended their sheep, farmers can jump into their muddy Land Rovers with the dogs in the back and trundle back to their firesides and high teas.

Look at the ruins of those farms. We have parked the car and walked across country to Tom's Hill and Larkbarrow. It doesn't take a great deal of imagination to give yourself some idea of the starkness and hardship in a life like that.

We had a cream tea in Simonsbath. We had a cream tea in nearly every other place we visited. It is what you do. Almost like shutting the gate.

We visited Lee Abbey, just outside Lynton. When we lived there, it used to play host to a variety of Christian holiday gatherings. Just below, we also visited Lee Bay, and disported ourselves on the beach in as few clothes as the weather would permit – which was not very often.

We ate, and drank, rather better in Challacombe, in *The Black Venus*. They boasted a car park – luxury. But it still rained – normality. The obvious thought occurs to you: how on earth did a Devon moorland pub acquire a name redolent of ancient mythology? And not just any old goddess – a politically correct goddess. As for how it got that name, there, as Mr. Holmes would have said, you move into deep waters.

The (inconsistently) informative Mr. Google talks, under the heading of 'Black Venus', about a Hottentot woman who was brought all the way from South Africa, and exhibited in some kind of freak show. Her name was Sarah Baartmann. Her surroundings were Dutch. Her sobriquet was the sort of cringing cliché one would expect from the media of any western country at pretty well any time since the eighteenth century. You know, any successful runner from Holland becomes The Flying Dutchman; any Slavonic con artist becomes the Bouncing Czech. Sarah was female, she was on show, so she must be an eyeful. Any 'native' from Africa was bound to be black. Hence, therefore, inevitably, she became 'The Black Venus'.

Oddly, she was unusually well endowed in the area of the buttocks, which, if nothing else, makes a change from the old Page 3 girls of the *Sun*. At any rate, she followed the sort of career one would expect for an uneducated black woman exhibited as some kind of curiosity to gaping nineteenth-century English society, which hardly saw an African once in a blue moon. She died in poverty in Paris in 1815, aged about thirty-odd. By a coincidence which also has a touch of freakishness about it, she died on 29th December. And, as I write this chapter, the date is 29th December. I didn't arrange this; I found out about Sarah's death not half an hour ago.

Now, if she did become a celebrity (she certainly travelled widely in her 'exhibitions'), it would make sense that places like pubs would adopt such an evocative name, as an aid to trade – cashing in on that celebrity. But the *Black Venus* in Challacombe claims, or the brochures say, that the Challacombe hostelry is the only place in England to bear that title. Odd.

But what a thing to come across: a remote moorland pub in Darkest Devon which has a name suggestive of a black African woman with large buttocks.

It's a bit difficult to follow that. So instead of trying to select a single 'wonder' which might be able to stand up to our Sarah, I shall simply offer a collection of tiny items, and hope to wear Sarah down with sheer numbers.

So let's go first to Winsford, which has a politician for its big name. There is a plaque up for public view which announces that Winsford was the birthplace of Ernest Bevin. Ernest Bevin? Oh, yes – one of the great political names of the 1930's and 1940's. A formidable union leader, a legendary Minister of Labour in the wartime coalition government, and a most unlikely Foreign Minister afterwards. But highly respected. It was said of him that it needed prodigious efforts to get him to agree to anything, but that, once he had given his word, you could stake your life on it. How many politicians would you fancy doing that with today?

He could also be devastatingly outspoken with the commonest of remarks. He was once on the edge of a conversation in which the participants were discussing the merits and demerits of a political opponent of Ernie's. Somebody observed, 'The trouble is that he's his own worst enemy.'

'Not while I'm alive he ain't,' grunted Ernie.

Ernie's career took him away from Devon. Others, with a successful career, chose to come here. Southey, Coleridge, and Wordsworth we have already mentioned. Paul McCartney bought property on the Moor. The Liberal leader Jeremy Thorpe lived in Cobbaton. Nowadays Cobbaton has to be content with a museum of military vehicles as a claim to fame. The comedian Dave Allen had a holiday home in Trentishoe. I bumped into him once in a garage in Lynton. As is often the case, he was smaller than you imagined he would be. Amiable though – a dip of the head and a wry smile; you half expected him to tell you a funny story while you waited for the mechanic's verdict.

Then there are the 'open air' sites. Like Watersmeet – an evocative confluence of rivers, as the name suggests. Lynmouth itself (quite apart from its hill) has its attractions – a Rhenish tower (what is so special about things 'Rhenish'?), a harbour, a confusion of shops selling the sort of things they imagine every visitor to Devon wants to buy – sweaters, pompoms, waterproofs (which tells you something about Devon weather, as if you didn't already know), boots, leatherwork, basketwork, and acres of souvenirs, which clutter shelves in one shop out of two, and which no doubt are taken away to clutter mantelpieces all over England. And teashops, don't forget – we all have to eat our cream teas somewhere.

The highest point on Exmoor is Dunkery Beacon. We went there too. Parked at the bottom and walked up an admittedly not very fearsome slope to the top. The trouble was that Stephen was a babe in arms, and that was how he made the trip – in my arms, all the way up and, unavoidably of course, all the way down. The sort of outing you remember.

For a county which is thought of as remote and rural (which it is) and therefore uninteresting (which it isn't), there were so many things worth seeing, and we certainly did not exhaust the list.

Torrington (sorry, '*Great* Torrington') isn't much to look at, but it lays claim to the site of a battle in the Civil War. Most towns can claim that they have a manor house somewhere or other nearby which was besieged, or which Cromwell knocked about a bit, but not many can claim actual battles. Torrington is also is home to a factory of world renown which makes practically everything for eating, drinking, and ornamenting – in glass. Fasten your cheque book before entering.

Just outside Torrington is a site where they grow every type, style, and colour of rose you can think of, and a lot more you have never heard of. So if, by chance, you are a local historian who is also a rose-lover, and you're looking for a vase to put the roses in, you can't do much better than Torrington (sorry again – 'Great' Torrington).

Then there are the places which do not have a rose cornucopia for sale or offer handblown glass cocktail-stirrers, but which you feel tempted to visit simply because of their names. Try Alverdiscott, (and hundreds of other 'cotts' all over the place), Woolfardisworthy (pronounced 'Woolsery'), Woody Bay, Stag's Head, Cheriton Fitzpaine down in the south (promise of Norman feudal heritage), Westward Ho! (don't forget the exclamation mark), Snapper, Bray*ford* (stress on the second syllable), Sheepwash, Chittlehamholt – one could line a chapter with them. Some turn out to be a disappointment; some are a treat, often not for the reason for which you made the visit.

Venture out on to the Moor: (real Injun country), and you can find (if you search diligently) Pinkworthy Pond (pronounced 'Pinkery'), Brendon Two Gates, Great Ferny Ball, Mole's Chamber (as I narrated in Chapter 5), and Five Barrows Cross (where the local public school start their annual cross-country run, the *Exmoor* – nine miles of it).

North Devon still has not exhausted its store of surprises. I have now lived in North Devon for over forty years. I can do a drive today of, say thirty or forty miles, and still I find myself passing signposts with names on them that I have never heard of.

Finally, I would like to mention the village of Selworthy, not far from Porlock. Not simply because it is famous, which it is. Or because it is beautiful and well preserved, which it also is. It is because we had a most memorable evening there.

Mrs. Coates sang in one or two local choirs. One Christmas, the choirmaster, Mr. Fordred, laid on a carol service in Porlock. It was a fair step, but Mrs. Coates was keen, we had a tough car, and it was the end of the school term, so we gave it a go. And of course the boys were all for it, because it meant a journey, and, even better, a late night.

I have no clear recollection of the actual service, except that it was a pleasant experience, as all carol services are. No, it was what happened afterwards. Mr. Fordred lived in Selworthy, in one of the many chocolate-box thatched cottages that enhanced the village. He had prepared an evening of log fires, mince pies, mulled wine, and a host of other goodies, and he invited the whole choir back to enjoy it, very kindly including our three boys, and me. This was especially welcome, because churches in winter are not especially cockles-of-the-heart-warming places. And it was a miserable night anyway – chilly and foggy.

I can not pick out individual details, but I still remember clearly the Christmas cheer, the good company, the splendid open fire, and the warmth and the glow (in every sense) that engulfed the evening. Mr. Fordred made the boys espccially welcome, and they had no time to be shy or retiring. Stephen particularly could not have been more than three, but he remembers it clearly.

And I think we all remember the drive back home – right across the Moor. It was late; it was dark (obviously); it was chill. We couldn't go fast because of the fog. The bends ambushed you like trolls in the wood. It demanded a good deal of concentration. But we built up a fair fug with the heater full on. Nobody complained. There was something of the explorer's adventure about the journey. All in all, for a great variety of reasons, a most satisfactory evening.

20

Fathering

Being an Austrian emperor would not be everyone's cup of tea. Some people may have been envious of the privilege, and covetous of the riches, but two weeks in the job would have taught them that there was a down side, which could be almost crushing. As Emperor Franz Joseph is supposed to have observed, 'You have to be born to it.'

Stephen was born to New Mill. Not *in* it, but precious close. Mrs. Coates endured a pregnancy in an old building with very few modern conveniences, no metalled road, and no telephone. Towards the end Miss Blackmore used to entertain her in her cottage up at Caffyn's on many afternoons – just in case. Well, as a retired health visitor, she would have known what to do. In fact, if the circumstances had so dictated, I'm sure would have made a perfectly sound job of delivering the infant. In the event, proceedings began late at night, and it was a case of squeezing her (not Miss Blackmore) into the old Land Rover and bouncing her up New Mill Lane to the cottage hospital in Lynton. And she was *very large*. In a five-foot woman, there isn't much scope for storing a nine-pound baby except to push him out forwards. There was no danger that you would not have seen her coming.

Luckily, by mid-afternoon on the next day, he had arrived. I wasn't there. The fashion for fathers being on hand, masked and sweating, to witness every movement and to hear every imprecation, had not yet taken on very widely. And I was not a modern father. I spent most of that afternoon up on Exmoor, sitting in the Land Rover, and gazing at moorland speckled with the remnants of a scrappy snowfall. Round about half-past four I thought, 'She should have had it by now'. This was not random guessing which betrayed my ignorance of obstetrics. I knew my wife; one of her favourite phrases was 'let's get on'. Once she had decided to have the baby, there was going to be no hanging around. (I believe she arrived early even at her own birth.) In fact my estimate had been a trifle 'under'. I arrived at the hospital to find Mrs. Coates sitting up in bed and wolfing sandwiches as if her life depended on it. 'Well,' she said, 'it doesn't half give you an appetite.'

She was so lively and animated that, for a moment, one would have been forgiven for wondering whether she had had a baby at all. But she had. All was well; he (it was a boy) was in the next room – a sort of new-born nursery, I suppose. So, naturally, I went to have a look.

Nothing especially remarkable. Like so many new arrivals, he looked like Edward G. Robinson. (If you don't know who Edward G. Robinson was, he was a Hollywood actor who became famous for gangster parts, and whose face looked like a new-born baby's – all spread and squashed.)

There was a small card attached to the cot. It said 'James Coates'. This needs explaining.

My name, as the title page shows, is Berwick Coates. My middle name is 'Manchee'. My father's middle name was 'Manchee'. My grandfather's wife's maiden name was 'Manchee'. It was common in those days, and for all I know is not uncommon now, for fathers to perpetuate their wife's family name among the Christian names of their offspring. In our family it was bestowed only on the eldest son.

I was well into my forties before I discovered that my father had not in fact been the eldest son. My grandfather lost all his first four children (again, sadly, all too common in those days). So my father was the eldest *surviving* son, and he got the 'Manchee'.

My grandfather and his brother had married two sisters, Connie and Minnie Manchee. His brother also continued the tradition by giving the family name to *his* son Conrad.

You should be now be saying to yourself, 'What an odd name.'

And I'm not surprised. 'Manchee' is not English. Well, it wasn't originally; it was French. A family member did some research. Apparently the family's name was 'Monchy', possibly even 'de Monchy'. In the sixteenth century one of them converted to the Protestant Church – in other words became a Huguenot, along, obviously, with his family.

As they lived in a Catholic country, they got persecuted, so Jean de Monchy emigrated to England. To London – Spitalfields – where they set up business as silk weavers. Like many persecuted minorities, they had to be well organised to survive. They ran their own hospital, where they kept detailed records. That is how we know so much about the family Monchy.

As you may guess, with the passage of time, the name evolved. 'Monchy' became 'Manchée', with the acute accent. In time again, the accent disappeared as an English pronunciation asserted itself. The family was prolific, and successful. Over the years it could boast at least two clergymen and a lord mayor of Bristol.

By the mid-to-late nineteenth century there was a Samuel Manchee, a chemist, who had two daughters, Connie and Minnie. They married the two brothers Coates, James and John, or Jim and Jack, as they were known in the family.

All this may or may not be fascinating, but it cut no ice with a little boy called 'Berwick', who thought that one funny Christian name was quite enough to be going on with. I got teased enough about the 'Berwick', so I kept as quiet as I could about the 'Manchee'. (Whether my father had suffered from the same embarrassment I don't know, because it never occurred to me to ask him.)

Why – on earth – 'Berwick'? Well, I don't want to interfere with the flow, but I had better explain. When my mother was a teenager, a man in the office where she worked had a nephew called 'Berwick', and she remembered thinking at the time what an interesting name it was. Then she forgot about it. Over a decade later, she had a difficult labour with me; we both nearly died. When she was just about able to take notice, the nurse said, 'Congratulations, Mrs. Coates. It's a boy. What are you going to call him?'

Out of the deep subconscious, like a long-submerged log, rose that name again.

'Berwick.'

When she had more fully recovered, the nurse said, 'By the way, you said "Berwick", but of course you meant "Derek", didn't you?'

My mother replied promptly and firmly, post-natal fever and all, 'I meant nothing of the kind; I meant "Berwick".' Whether she was just being cussed or not, she stuck to 'Berwick', and that was what I had to carry through primary school.

That was my mother's contribution to my educational life. My father's was, as I said, 'Manchee'. 'Berwick Manchee Coates' – what a mouthful.

Well, like my mother with 'Berwick', I did not give the 'Manchee' a great deal of thought after surviving primary school. I grew up, and 'Manchee' ceased to be a cross.

Now, years later, there I was, in the Lynton Cottage Hospital, with my firstborn in my arms. Just like my mother, I found that submerged log rising again. I remember the thought going through my head, 'This may be your only chance, mate.'

So 'Manchee' it was to be.

That was not the end of it. I went into the nursery, where the name label still hung from the bars of the cot. It said 'James Coates'.

You would think that I would have found that especially acceptable, because my grandfather was 'James'. Not so. That confounded submerged log rose again. . .

When I was nine, I had to go to the dentist. (You'll see the point in a minute.) It was a school dentist – rapid, conveyor-belt stuff. I had a tooth taken out with barely a warning, and I am not sure to this day whether I had enough gas, because I kept some memory of the procedure. I remember being conscious of an invasion of the body which was almost traumatic. I have since found that that experience gave me the means of understanding, if only a little, why women find rape such a shock.

However, I was feeling pretty raw afterwards. The local library was next door to the clinic, and, as we had to pass it on the way home, my mother suggested that it might be an idea to join and take a book or two home, as a sort of therapy. I was a bookish kid, so it was apt.

There was a junior section. You were allowed to choose one book of fiction and one of non-fiction. I took out a western novel called *Across Texas* (which contained a very dramatic bit about a tarantula), and an account of Scott's South Pole expedition, called *No Surrender*. Well, I said I was bookish. Don't ask me why I should have remembered those titles; I just do.

But it's what I did on my second visit that is relevant. The novel I picked off the shelf was about a young American mining engineer who in 1902 was sent to prospect for gold in Siberia of all places. It was called, unsurprisingly, *Siberian Gold*.

Only one other book has ever bowled me over more than that one (*The Wind in the Willows*). It had a great story, some great characters, two villains for the price of one, and a scattering of magical words in Russian that I speedily added to my vocabulary. *Mujik* was the obvious one. Many of us know what a *mujik* is, and if you are good at geography you will know all about the *taiga* and the *tundra*. But I bet you don't know what a *chenovnik* is. Or a *hishnik*. Or a *kinjal*. I do.

I took that book out of the library – oooohhh, a score of times. To my great joy, I discovered that there was a sequel, called *Kubrik the Outlaw*. I read that umpteen times too. Years later, I discovered both in second-hand bookshops. They are among my most treasured possessions.

Even more of a coincidence, I discovered, only last month, thanks to the internet, that there is a sequel to the sequel, and I am reading it now.

What has all this to do with the birth of my son? If you recall, I spoke of 'that confounded submerged log' rising for the third time. In *Siberian Gold*, the young American mining engineer was called 'Stephen Wyld'. I had no idea of it at the time, but at the age of nine I had laid down the log that was to surface nearly thirty years later in a ward in a cottage hospital in Devon.

194

I took off the card, crossed out 'James', and wrote in 'Stephen Manchee'.

What did the recipient think of all this? Well, when he began to take notice, he didn't mind the 'Stephen', but he hated the 'Manchee'. So much so that for several years he dropped the 'Manchee' altogether. Oddly, he quite liked the name 'James' – the name that never was.

About two years ago, he became a father himself – quite late. And what did he call his son? 'James George Manchee Coates'. (George was the name of his wife's father.) I don't know if there is some kind of moral there, but there may well be yet another 'submerged log'.

So Stephen was born a Devonian. The other two were not. Until he was three, Stephen had never known any other home. The others had. New Mill entered their lives and their memories – certainly they reminisce about it very readily. Indeed I am indebted to both of them for material in the writing of this book. But with Stephen, I fancy it was almost a case of New Mill entering his blood. He is not sentimental about it, and has now lived over half his life out of Devon, but I think that those first three years laid down something that Christopher and Martin could not possibly have had. (We are back to the submerged log again.)

There is no judgment implied; it is simply a fact. When one considers the circumstances, it would be rather odd if such were not the case. You are what you are; you cannot change how you started.

To their great credit, the boys accepted him totally, and did their fair share of minding, looking after, and generally watching out for him. When we said 'the boys', by the way, we always meant Christopher and Martin, never all three. And so it remained. Rather like the way we continued to refer to the new Land Rover as – wait for it – 'the new Land Rover', long after it had lost the sheen of youth. Right up to the day we sold it at fifteen years old. Similarly, in the house we moved to after leaving New Mill, we had a small section on the end which contained an old toilet and a – well, just a space. I used to do a spot of DIY there, so it was christened 'the

195

outside workshop', despite the fact that there was no built-in bench or tool rack, and it wasn't even outside; it was built on to the house.

When 'the boys' were not taken up with looking after Stephen, they found him very useful – as a stooge, a fall guy, a catspaw, a guinea-pig, a mascot, or any other useful role which might enhance whatever activity they got up to. More of that later.

I should imagine that a health visitor would have found our circumstances a mite inadequate for the nurturing of a newly-arrived infant, and, later, of a small boy. I have already mentioned the absence of central heating and double glazing, and the solitary plastic pipe which brought water down from the spring. (Remember? The cattle-with-liver-fluke spring.) We did however boil all the water he consumed, just to make sure.

We took steps also to protect him from the fire, which was a good deal bigger than average. We went to Richards and Jones and bought a massive structure half as big as a chicken run which could have covered our fireplace twice. But when we moved into the other half, the fireplace was twice as big, so in the end we needed every inch of it.

We took advantage of every bit of help offered by neighbours. David Leworthy's wife Maureen lent us a playpen. Sturdy and sizeable, fitting for a farmer's wife. Certainly it contained Stephen very satisfactorily. Later on, he was able to take out a strut or two from his cot, but he never made any impression on Maureen's playpen.

It was in the playpen that he reached one of the great milestones in a baby's life: he stood up for the first time (using the playpen as scaffolding of course). Well, that was fine, and he felt the natural sense of achievement. The trouble was, he had not looked far enough forward. He had mastered the knack of standing up, but he had forgotten to rehearse the procedure for sitting down. Puzzled, baffled, and finally quite distressed, he turned a tearful face towards us, still clutching the bars of the playpen. We had to rescue him.

When he was *very* small, the wife of the Parracombe vet lent us a carry-cot. We never owned a pram. Pushing a pram up New Mill

Lane for a gentle afternoon promenade was simply not on. There is an Ancient Greek legend about a chap called Sisyphus, whose eternal punishment in Hades was to have to roll a great stone up a steep hill. But each time he was on the very verge of the summit, it slipped, and rolled all the way down the hill again. Guess what he had to do then. If Mrs. Coates had attempted propelling a pram up to Caffyn's, Sisyphus would have welcomed her as a kindred sufferer. We must have had a folding push-chair to put in the car. I have no recollection of buying one. If we didn't, I suppose we must have borrowed that too, but again I have no recollection of the kind lender.

Even more potentially dangerous than the fire was of course the river. Looking back, I don't recall either of us lying awake at night wondering how on earth we were going to manage. For twelve months or so, obviously, he was not going to go anywhere much. Then there was the usual twelve-to-eighteen-month period when hands were on offer while the subject crawled or tottered from one object of curiosity to the next.

Thereafter, he had two worthy guardians who rarely left him when they were out of doors. They rarely had to be warned about this, because, out of doors, there were so many absorbing things to do which involved him. As I explained, they were in such regular need of a stooge. If they weren't there, James and Andrew from up the valley were. As often as not, he had four near-constant minders.

All of them had enough common sense to be wary of the water, and in bad weather they never went near it. I like to think that we gave them the impression that we *expected* them to be sensible, and so they always were. They learnt to have respect for the river. We never had a single incident of danger or drama. Martin fell in, yes, but it was low, and he had only himself to blame, and he speedily kept hauling himself out – till he ran out of dry clothes and came indoors to put himself to bed.

Only once did Stephen give us cause for worry, and it was nothing to do with the river. We wanted him in for tea or something, and we went outside to call him. He did not answer. We tried loudly. No reply. We went out to the back of the house and tried again. Still no reply. We covered the ground all about the house. Nothing.

Now we *were* concerned. Suddenly every feature of New Mill, which we had got so used to that we rarely thought about them, took on the guise of a potential threat – water, brambles, wire fences, ditches, a collapsing bank – there was no shortage.

Well, he wasn't hurt; he wasn't in danger; he wasn't lost. He was playing a joke on us. He thought it would be a great wheeze to stay silent and create a bit of mystery. In short, an innocent bit of mischief. The serious faces of Mum and Dad, and the even more serious lecture he received from them, took him aback. He never did it again.

He was not short of other adventures. James from up the valley had a mechanical bent. I have mentioned the motor bike he put together. When he was about fifteen, he came into possession of a 'proper' motor bike. Understandably he was the object of a great deal of interest from our three. I don't think Christopher or Martin ever drove it, but James used to give Stephen rides on the petrol tank.

It was an orange bike. Stephen was only three when we left New Mill, but he has a very clear recollection of it. Well, if you had been astride a fully-grown-up motor bike when you were three, you would probably have a clear recollection too. Long, long after that, after we had been away from New Mill for over thirty years, we paid a visit. We knew that James' family now owned it, and rented it out for holiday guests (having done it up of course – you wouldn't have attracted many visitors with paraffin stoves, black plastic pipes, and Mole's Chamber).

We drove down the modern version of New Mill Lane that James had built; we parked, and wandered across the front of the house. Suddenly we heard the roar of a motor bike, turned, and there was James, coming from his own house up the valley, and *he was astride an orange motor bike*. Stephen said it was almost ghostly.

Christopher and Martin could not offer such mechanised sophistication as that. Their own ambitions were more modest. They started with one wheel. Martin had a small bicycle when he first arrived, and was fond of riding it here, there, and everywhere. He took it into his head to attempt a sort of 'ski-jump' ride over a small wall beside the main path. As with his ventures into paddling, and bombing boats, he came unstuck once again, and virtually wrote the bike off.

But they salvaged one wheel from the wreckage, and fashioned a vehicle for Stephen to play at motor bikes with. He loved doing 'wheelies' with it.

Not to be outdone I entered the fray as well. I had a mower. Not a very good one. The garden wasn't a very good one either. Stones lurked near the surface, and you would look at it for a long time before you thought of a billiard table. Still, I worked with my Heath-Robinson machine to make it look vaguely civilised.

Stephen was very taken with this mower. Clearly, at three, he could not aspire to driving it. So something had to be done. Back to the workshop. Even if you weren't any great mechanic, New Mill was the sort of place where you could always find enough scrips and scraps which, with the aid of patience, bits of Meccano, and a lot of luck, could be cobbled together to produce a distant resemblance to what you had in mind (so long as you had a vivid imagination).

So a regular sight on the estate was the Chief Engineer puffing behind a throaty Briggs and Stratton, and making a modest impression on the local savannah, and, a few yards behind, an Assistant Engineer pushing a miniature version and making the appropriate glottal noises in default of a petrol engine.

However, Stephen was not merely a recipient; he made contributions to the life of New Mill on his own account. I have just mentioned the time he made us think he was lost or injured. For all the risk-worthy features of New Mill, that was about the only time in three years that we were afraid lest something had happened to any of them.

Martin famously fell in the water – three times – but we were all around. Christopher fell and broke his wrist, but once again we were there, and any boy could have fallen and broken his wrist anywhere.

Stephen added to the atmosphere by managing to fall *up* the stairs. I had recently added some stair carpet to the palatial furnishing of the house, and I suppose he simply wasn't used to such comforts. At any rate he tripped, fell forwards, and struck his chin on a tread, which caused his jaws to close rapidly. He bit his tongue, but not in the usual place near the tip. This was right back, so far that, when you looked inside his mouth, through the streaming blood (which was frightening us much more than it was frightening him), you had to squint hard to see the hole.

We were not sure whether this merited a visit to the cottage hospital. By good fortune, Miss Blackmore was either visiting at the time, or arrived shortly afterwards. Ex- health visitor, remember? She took one look and said we had nothing to worry about, and – even more surprising – we needed to do nothing.

'No, no – it will heal quickly. The mouth is one of the warmest, healthiest places in the body. Let it be.'

So we did. And it did.

Rather more tiresome were his midnight dramas; he became a martyr to croup. It was a case of lugging him down to the kitchen, boiling water by the gallon, and trying to get as much steam into him as we could.

Sometimes it wasn't easy to get him to sleep afterwards. I had to resort to story-telling. I tried to relate the most boring anecdotes I could think up, hoping that it would have the same effect that my most tedious lessons would have on my classes. One wearisome night, it wouldn't work. There he was, *standing up* in the cot, alive and agog, demanding to know what happened next, and there was father, sitting and swaying, struggling merely to keep his eyes open, never mind to think up the next episode.

Like all infants, he was rarely eager to go to sleep, even when he was fully fit and had had an energetic day. Must have been the New Mill air. Which was odd, because we noticed that, when we had visitors staying overnight on their first visit to Devon, the air regularly made their eyelids droop not all that long after dinner.

The boys were very good at helping us out with 'saying

goodnight', but it often necessitated more than one trip, by each of us. It was here that two names were coined. He christened Christopher 'Gubby'. Martin was called 'Nami'. We never found out why. A regular night-time ritual was the distant treble, faint but insistent from on high: 'Can Gubby come up?' And, of course, ten minutes after Christopher had done his duty, 'Can Nami come up?'

How do children make up names? There is scope here for a treatise on infant creative word-coining. Should be good for a post-graduate thesis and doctorate in some red-brick college of education.

Many, of course, are mere approximations to what the child *thinks* he has heard. So Stephen's version of 'bumblebee' was 'bimbombee', which is fair enough. A 'butterfly' became a 'buttonflower', which has a rural, Beatrix-Potter charm of its own. Pollyanna's mother told us that she too had been similarly creative: when she held out her hand for the flannel at the night-time bath, Elise would hold it out and say, ' 'Ere y'are'. So the flannel thereafter became the 'eeyare'.

But others, like the best nicknames, defy analysis. I have just quoted 'Gubby' and 'Nami'. Stephen's best effort, though (well, *we* thought so), was his treatment of the word 'trousers'. 'Trajels.' (Pronounced 'trayjls'.) By what alchemy of transposition or mis-pronunciation did he produce 'trajels'?

Of course we all fastened on to this, and used to quote him. Slowly, what began as a joke and a tease hardened into habit. We came to use the word 'trajels' without thinking, with a perfectly straight face. 'Go and put your trajels on.' It entered New Mill vernacular, along with 'fucshials' and 'japonical' and ' Mole's Chamber'.

Similarly James from up the valley got the treatment. James, who was a tall lad for his age, would put his head round the door, and catch sight of Stephen who was looking him straight in the kneecaps. He would look down and say, 'Hallo, big Steve.'

Stephen would reply, 'Hallo, Drames.'

'Drames' is not a misprint; that was Stephen's name for him. Another word for the New Mill glossary.

I have related all but one of the episodes I remember (with the boys' assistance). No doubt there were others, either which we have all forgotten, or which they have seen fit not to tell me, for obvious reasons. If parents were to know absolutely everything their children got up to, the world would be much fuller of cases of apoplexy or cardiac arrest.

When I was at primary school myself, we used to pass some huge advertisement hoarding on our way home. Some of the planking had come off, leaving a bare trellis-work of battening underneath. One could, if one were so disposed, climb up this trellis-work right to the top, a matter of at least thirty feet.

Some of us were indeed so disposed. Indeed, one daring soul not only climbed up to the top; he hoicked his leg over and came down the other side. I cannot imagine what induced me to tackle this Fairbanks feat. A dare, I suppose. The things we do in order to show that we are not scared, when in fact we are terrified.

I was a wimp. I never went down on toboggans. I never slid on ice across playgrounds. I never climbed trees. Yet, there I was, going up this damned hoarding. Not over the top, I admit. But just to the top was enough. Even at this distance of time, I am still incredulous. If my mother had ever found out, the lectures and sermons would have been dire. If she had actually seen me, it would have done for her.

I rather fancy that if either of us had witnessed what I am about to relate, it might have had a similar seismic effect on any fond father or mother.

The wonder is not that we did not see it; you can't keep an eye on them all the time. No, the wonder is that we were either too unobservant to notice the obviously lengthy preparations, or too dense to deduce what they were going to lead up to.

Another mark of the influence of New Mill on the boys' lives. There was so much space; there were so many features that you did not find in the average garden; there were so many nooks, crannies, corners, dens, and hidey-holes. The sort of places where all red-blooded boys just like to be. We couldn't be everywhere. As

I said, we trusted them. And we had the advantage over millions of residents in ordinary homes in ordinary roads near ordinary shops and roads. We did not have to worry about traffic. We were not frequented by regular passers-by, among whom could be the occasional unsavoury customer.

By the same token, we did not have to be concerned about what the boys might get up to which could annoy neighbours. There weren't any – not in the normal sense. Nobody complained if we made noises, bonfires, dams, walls, sheds, or anything else much. It was a bit like being on the American frontier.

So we had had motor-bikes, mowers, one-wheeled gadgets, mud-caked outside toilets, boat-bombing, camps, secret trails, Guy Fawkes nights, fishing expeditions, total immersion, and fascination with septic tanks (we once caught Stephen, beside the tip tray of the filter bed, dipping his flannel in the 'water' and 'washing' his face).

So the stage was set for the boys' *magnum opus*, their *chef d'oeuvre*, their *pièce de résistance*, their masterstroke – the go-kart.

I have no idea who thought it up. It is quite likely that they don't remember either. Like Topsy, it probably 'just growed'. I must confess that I too don't remember much. I have picked all their brains, and even now a full picture has not emerged from the thicket of fond memory and legend.

However, it must have been of significance to them, and it figures regularly in their reminiscence sessions.

It was to be a major advance on one-wheel 'motor-bikes' and miniature mowers. It was to have more than one measly wheel. It was to have a steering mechanism. It was to generate some appreciable speed. One version of the fable claims that it was also to have some kind of 'cabin' for the 'driver'. A solo driver – their engineering skill, resources, budget, hopes, and imagination did not take them as far as a passenger.

Clearly they could not make a whole undercarriage. My sole contribution to the project was to suggest that all sorts of junk found its way to the municipal tip. Christopher made the very sensible, and relevant point that municipal tips were not wide-open treasure troves for small boys, for obvious reasons of health if for no other.

Asking permission therefore was likely to produce a negative response, and then where would we be? Never ask a question if you are not prepared for the possible answer. So Alexander here cut the Gordian Knot. How would it be if we didn't say a word and just helped ourselves? After all, the welfare of the municipality of Lynton and Lynmouth was not going to be put in jeopardy by the removal of one rusty set of clapped-out pram wheels. And what the eye did not see. . .

Christopher was not sure about this; all his conformist instincts rose to the surface. And I don't blame him. I don't think it was the punishment if we were to be caught; it would be the shame. I am no rebel either, but I did a thorough risk assessment, and fancied that we were in with a good chance of getting away with it, especially if we cracked the joint very early in the morning, even before the dustmen got busy.

I put on a bold face and told Chris that he had no need to worry. Village policemen were not in the habit of making dawn patrols of municipal tips, and there was a good chance that dustmen were not endowed with the power of arrest. There was also the chance that, if the worst happened, we could leg it out of sight.

So we did it. We came away with a set of old push-chair wheels, like triumphant archaeologists after discovering a new civilisation. The smug satisfaction was tinged with just a small dash of relief – for both of us.

After all that we didn't use them. One of the boys discovered a small jungle of farm machinery in the corner of a field – dead, rusty, and overgrown. My contribution this time was not larceny; it was a phone call to the farmer to ask. Well, there was no way we could have moved it all.

His reply was both a relief and a challenge. He didn't want it, but was not going to move it for them. If the boys could saw off the bits they wanted, they were welcome.

Christopher says it took them three days with small hacksaws, but they came away with not only a set of wheels but with some kind of steering mechanism as well.

This is a good example of what a place like New Mill could do for boys. There they were, totally absorbed, grinding away with modest little hacksaws, at a ruined set of abandoned machinery in the overgrown corner of a distant field – for three whole days. All because it seemed a good idea. All because their imagination had been fired. Were it not for New Mill, the circumstances would never have arisen for them even to get the idea.

I was not privy to the details of the construction, or of the launch, for that matter. What actually happened has filtered through to me over the years. No doubt various frills were added to the narrative with each telling. I could not therefore give a detailed running commentary of the actual itinerary of this vehicle. All I can do is piece together what scraps of reminiscence remain to make some kind of coherent account, and leave all other parents to contemplate how they themselves would have reacted if they had known in advance, or, worse, actually witnessed it.

The simplest approach is to outline what they planned to do. How close they came to success, and how close they came to disaster, we shall probably never know.

I ask you to picture for a moment the geography of this incident. New Mill Lane was steep – one in four at least. The further down you went, the rougher and stonier it became. And I don't mean gravel, or even chippings; I mean rocks which could jut several inches above the surface, and which you knew had nine-tenths of their mass below ground. Like icebergs.

In the middle of course was the raised line of grass and beaten earth thrown up by generations of tractors going up and down.

Near the bottom were two wicked bends, more rough and rocky than the rest. At the turn of the last bend, the lane overhung a drop to more rocks, straggling saplings, a forest of Russian rhubarb, and the water. There was no fence, wire, or barrier of any kind.

Apparently what they proposed to do was to sit Stephen in the go-kart at the higher bend, give him a shove, and launch him towards the lower one, trusting to luck and his steering skill to avoid the raspberry canes on one side and the precipice down to Ilkerton Water on the other, so that he would make a perfect three-point landing in front of the house.

To be sure, they did not expect Stephen to do it all by instinct; they gave him a crash course (*le mot juste* if ever there was one) once they had seated him. Stephen remembers nothing of the ride, but he does remember his briefing very clearly. Christopher explained the mechanism. Because it was obvious to *him*, and he was explaining clearly, he assumed that it would be obvious and clear to a three-year-old. Stephen says he recalls vividly the thought going through his head while Christopher expounded with remorseless logic: he hadn't the faintest idea what Christopher was talking about. He says that his brother became a mite annoyed because he, Stephen, was not grabbing it straight off the bat.

To be honest, that is about all I can say with any certainty. Everyone's memory seems to get foggy after that. I know of course that Stephen did not get hurt, and did not get launched straight off the bend into the water. I don't know how long he managed to stay aboard. I don't know if Christopher's instructions suddenly fell into place under the stress of the actual descent (you know, rather like being in front of a firing squad: it concentrates the mind wonderfully). I don't know if the go-kart survived the ordeal. I don't know if they sent him down again, to make sure that he got it right in the end. But it all makes for splendid speculation.

We arrive therefore at the situation wherein the entertainment potential of this anecdote relies not on what actually happened, but one what people can imagine *could* have happened. And the ramifications were indeed dumbfounding.

Those of you who are particularly observant will have noticed that this chapter is the longest in the book. The natural reaction would be to put it down to paternal fondness. Well, you could make a case, I concede. But in all the conversations I have had with the boys about New Mill, these episodes appear the most frequently and consistently.

206

If I had skimped them, they would unfailingly have said, 'The go-kart and the wheelies – why didn't you write about. . . ?' whatever detail it was. So I hope I have satisfied all parties.

Finally, it needs recording that Stephen himself was the inspiration of this book. We were on the phone one day, talking of this and that, and New Mill came up – yet again. He said, 'You know, you must put down this stuff about New Mill, because if you don't, I shall forget, and I don't want to forget. My memory is terrible. And I was only two or three; you will remember things that went right past me. I don't want the picture to fade.'

Well, here is the picture, to the best of my ability. I hope it postpones the fading.

21

Leaving

There was an Ancient Greek philosopher called Heraclitus who worked himself into the history books by declaring that nothing ever stayed constant; everything was in a state of flux. We are not the person we were half an hour ago. The chair you are sitting in has declined infinitesimally since you sat in it. You cannot wade into the same river twice. And so on.

In the same way, New Mill after five years was not the house we had moved into five years before. Well, it is difficult to argue with that. I think it would have been depressing indeed if someone had been able to convince us that we had made no impression on New Mill at all. As for the river, I suppose it is unarguable that the water had changed, and was changing all the time. Nevertheless, that stream also had the quality of permanence, if not unchangeability. It was the constant underlying theme, the heartbeat, the permanent obbligato of our life there.

What was changing most, of course, was ourselves. Mr. and Mrs. Coates were getting older, though, let me stress, not all that much older. Five years in a life that is forty-plus years old is not a great deal. But it is if you are eleven and thirteen, and even more so if you are three.

I think, if you had asked any of us at almost any time during those five years what our plans were for the future, the answer would have been vague in the extreme. No doubt the boys had moments when they missed the comforts of suburbia. If the truth be told, such a thought crossed the minds of both parents from time to time.

But I hope I have been able to show that New Mill was an

absorbing place. School, work, mere living, and the house itself were usually enough to take up most of one's conscious thoughts.

Nevertheless, the boys were growing, as boys have a habit of doing. They were all three in the same bedroom. Stephen did not take up much room in his cot, and the other two had bunk beds. But Martin was now eleven, and Christopher was thirteen. Secondary school had added the problem of where to do one's homework.

We didn't make a conscious resolution, but, looking back, it was clear that Something would have to happen. We had had dreams, of course, and projects, and bright ideas. There had been cursory glances at property adverts in the local paper. We even went to give a few places the once-over. But I don't think the heart was in it. It just didn't seem right.

In the event, as in so many similar circumstances, it sort of crept up on us. It insinuated itself through the school grapevine. I heard one day, or saw an announcement on the Common Room notice board, that the council were offering a four-bedroomed house, detached, for a practising teacher in the Barnstaple area. Normally a four-bedroomed, detached house would not have merited a first thought, never mind a second one; it would have been right out of my range. If you had asked me two or three weeks before I saw that advert, I should have said that the chances of my obtaining occupation of a four-bedroomed detached house near Barnstaple were no better than had been my chances of acquiring a country cottage in Devon in the first place.

This one, though, like New Mill, was different. It was not for sale; it was for rental. Not only that; it was much nearer to my work. It was in a village only a mile away from my school. And of course the phrase about four bedrooms blazed away like a neon sign.

I made enquiries at the local education office. Was I eligible to apply? Yes, I was; it said 'practising teachers in the Barnstaple area'. No mention of distance, age, type of school, size of family, academic qualifications, experience – just 'practising teachers'. Well, that was me all right.

I made more enquiries. It lay on the main road between Barnstaple and Exeter, just outside the village of Bishop's Tawton. Right on the main road, as it transpired. Well, that was going to be a change from the moorland fastnesses of New Mill.

I submitted an application. My case was of course unanswerable: five years' devoted service to the county, growing family, much easier for me to get into work in bad weather and so to avoid being an imposition on colleagues who would have to take my lessons if I was snowed up – and so on and so on. (The fact that in five years we had never *been* snowed up I did not think relevant to the argument, naturally. As the senior civil servant would have said to his minister, they did not 'need to know' that.)

I waited. In the meantime, I did some asking around, and found out that there were three other applications besides mine, two of them from colleagues of my own school.

The grapevine sap ran again. One of those colleagues said she and her husband had changed their mind. The field narrowed to three. The other colleague found a house that he liked better and that he could afford to buy. Down to two. Finally, I heard that the fourth applicant was a teacher who had applied for a post in the area, and had been successful; he too had changed his mind – not about the house, but about the job – he didn't want it now. So obviously he didn't want the house either.

All I had to do then was to wait for the letter telling me that the house was mine. I got a letter all right, but it told me that my application had not been successful.

One convenient thing about rural local authorities is that you can usually get an interview with somebody important if you ask. I did, and I did. I got the Deputy Chief Education Officer. Not quite the *obergruppenführer,* but the next one down.

Understandably I was baffled, mystified, unable to understand. . . all right, I was cross, and I did my fair share of blustering and what-the-helling. What made me even crosser was that he would not argue, not even discuss. I felt I was shadow-boxing; all my spleen was vanishing into thin air. He simply sat there sucking his pipe.

'The situation has changed.'

I huffed and puffed again. The only animation he showed was to relight his pipe.

'The situation has changed.'

Then I had a bright idea. Well, it struck me as a bright idea.

'Would you be kind enough to arrange for me an interview with the Chief Education Officer?'

To his credit, he did.

I thought I was in with a faint chance: I had met this distant deity once or twice, and I was teaching his son. Chance or no chance, I had come this far; I might as well pursue this course to the very end. I had nothing to lose.

The following week, I met the CEO. I stated my case, trying hard this time not to huff and puff. He listened. I can't remember what he said. But a week later I received another letter to inform me that I was being offered the tenancy of School House, Bishop's Tawton.

The situation had changed.

I never found out what the decisive factor was in the *volte-face*. When I told the story to others, the commonest reaction was 'you scared him, that's what. It'll teach him that ordinary teachers like you are not going to be pushed around. Petty little dictators. The minute you called his bluff he caved in.'

Well, that is as may be. But my impression of this Deputy Chief Education Officer was that he did not look the sort of man who was going to be overawed by anything much. He had vast experience, and he was infuriatingly still throughout the encounter. He did not argue because he clearly did not think I was worth arguing *with*.

I once worked with a headmaster who was like that with irate parents. Mrs. Bumble would surge into his office breathing fire and brimstone because of some mortal offence suffered by her innocent son, and begin to detonate a verbal broadside. He did not argue; he did not comment; he simply listened. When Mrs. Bumble had talked herself to a standstill, he would reach into his desk, pull out a council form, take the top off his fountain pen, and say, 'Now, Mrs. Bumble, into which primary school would you like to have your son transferred?'

Well, anyway, I never found out. I had the house, and that was what mattered. All that remained was to organise the move, and also to change the boys' secondary school. They could not continue attending Ilfracombe Comprehensive. It would mean Barnstaple Comprehensive – or, as it became christened, the Park School. (Well, it was near the Park.)

Christopher was pretty phlegmatic about it. Or, if he was furious, he diplomatically did not tell me. He could look forward to a much bigger bedroom, with no chatty infant in a cot in the corner, so perhaps that played a part.

Martin was two years younger, and had just made the traumatic move from tiny Lynton Primary to the vastness of Ilfracombe Comp. It wasn't easy for an eleven-year-old. It never is. Now he would have to do it all over again. That did hurt.

However, there really was no argument. I did hover for a short while. Any head of household will pause a little as a rule, because it means a step in the dark, and he is responsible for, in my case, five people, and he knows that the other four are not going to look at it in the same way that he does. I think I was influenced by the comment a distant relative made when he saw School House (and he had seen New Mill). He raised an eyebrow or two and said, 'And he is *hesitating*?'

Well, we did it. And what did we move to? School House had been built in 1904, and there had been a bit of subsidence in the first decade or two. I stress that it has long since stopped, in case some eagle-eyed insurance agent should cast his eyes over this paragraph. But it meant that the house had more than its fair share of faint trapeziums in the doorways and window frames. (Or is it *trapezia*?) But even that had its advantages: no glib double-glazing salesman was going to talk us into buying much.

Because it was in effect a council house, the local authority had arranged for it to be decorated at intervals – quite long intervals, I suspect. It was done hurriedly, and it was done on the cheap, and I doubt if any clerk of the works came round to inspect. The result was that no sash windows were ever raised or lowered in the process.

When we got there, not a single window could be opened. They had to employ a chippy for a couple of days. Even then the trapeziums (or *trapezia*) interfered with the smooth raising and lowering. (A dozen years later, when Stephen was sixteen, the two of us tackled the whole exterior – two coats. This time they did send a man round to check up, and he was honest enough to admit that we had made a better job of it than his own men would have done.)

There was no central heating. Warmth and hot water came from a venerable Courier stove which had been installed in the place of an even more venerable black kitchen range. The aperture was keenly reminiscent of New Mill. As with New Mill too, drainage was by means of septic tank.

So at least the new house would hold few surprises.

One of them was something that had been absent from New Mill. As I said at the outset, many thousands of people have dreamed of a solid stone house with a large garden and roses round the door. New Mill had the stone and the large garden, but no roses round the door. School House did. Well, not exactly round the door, but all the way up a trellis only four or five yards from the door. So we only found our roses when we left New Mill.

That sentence could pass for a moral to the tale. It is almost poetic, quite by accident. It has a rhythm and pitch. Read it. We only found our roses when we left New Mill.

There is another parallel too. School House, like New Mill, was not short of disadvantages, but, like New Mill again, it did have one vital statistic in its favour. New Mill, if you remember, sold itself to me because the rent was two pounds a week. Eight years later, I was able to rent a four-bedroomed detached house, with shed, garage, parking, and large garden, for eighteen pounds a month. Think about that for 1975.

22

A House for all Seasons

So we moved. Did we look back over our shoulder much at New Mill? No, I don't think so. School House was bigger, and, taking things all round, more comfortable. It meant far less travel for me. It meant easy access to Barnstaple for Mrs. Coates. We had public facilities more easily available, although it was still several years before we had the phone installed. This may strike many as odd, because the phone these days is regarded as being as vital as a front door or a kitchen tap; you ask for the phone in the morning and the men come round in the afternoon. When I was growing up it could take weeks, even months. You lived in expectation, you talked about it, you naturally looked forward to it, you thought at times that it would never come. It was a bit like being pregnant.

So a delay did not strike me as particularly odd. We had a public phone up the road, which is what we had always been used to. (It is now a gaunt, derelict, mottled-red wreck.) The three-hundred-yard walk to get there was an inconvenience sometimes, but not a hardship. If it had been, I suppose I should have done something about it earlier. It just shows you how times and attitudes change. No householder today, I'm sure, would tolerate such a situation without a very good reason.

We had neighbours, though we did not in fact see a great deal of them. At right-angles to us was a small row of terrace houses, and we got to know the names of only two of the occupants. At one end was an old lady who apparently owned half Bishop's Tawton, but was practically a recluse. In the middle was an even older lady whom we christened Mrs. Clackit. You know, black bonnet, permanent pinafore, spindly legs, next to nothing to say, and never moving – only pottering. When she was taken ill some years later and had to be transferred into hospital, we heard that she was given the first bath she had ever had in her life. The trauma did for her. No more Mrs. Clackit.

At the other end was a couple who were indeed helpful. Mrs. was somewhat formidable – arms folded like a wrestler in a sports photograph and permanently gleaming eyes. You got the feeling that if she had ever been starving in a siege, she would have eaten you. But she was kind and meant well. Mr. was much more friendly – according to Mrs. Coates a sight too friendly. He had a habit in conversation of insinuating one of his hands round ladies' waists and giving a gentle squeeze just above the hip. What made it more disconcerting was what we found out about his job. He worked at the local mortuary, laying out the bodies. . . Exactly – where had those hands been just before he gave a squeeze?

We had so much to occupy us. Think of all the jobs that need doing when you move house. The boys had their new schools. Mrs. Coates continued for a while with her post as school secretary at Lynton, so it was she who had the commuting now.

It was a much easier house to visit, so we had more conversations with people coming in. I hasten to point out that it was not anything like the Archers – you know, with half of Ambridge forever 'dropping in' through the never-locked door. Nevertheless, we did see more of the human race.

The garden was big enough to allow plenty of space for play, and it was adjacent to a farmer's field, with, nearby, a sort of thicket, and, below that, a railway line and the River Taw. The boys still had things to beware of, and places to have adventures in.

Gradually, as we tamed School House (though, like New Mill, it never came to heel completely, and it still hasn't), we found time to sit back and reminisce. . .

At New Mill, we did things; we created things; there seemed to be so much space in which to do so. Nowadays one would say that we 'developed skills'. Christopher found his fishing, and showed a great aptitude with modelling kits. Most people turn the box over to give a cursory glance at the instructions on the back, get stuck in, get stuck when they *are* in, then get fed up with the thing when it won't do what they want. As often as not it doesn't get finished.

Not so with Christopher. He read it all – everything. He did what it said. Result – success. He had little patience with those who couldn't be bothered and ended up frustrated. It was the most transparent common sense to him. It was some kind of gift denied to most ordinary mortals. He actually read the instructions; better, he actually understood them; best of all, he could follow them.

Martin did put things together; he also liked taking things apart, to find out how they worked. According to Mrs. Coates, a toy which he had been given when he was two lasted about half an hour in one piece. It was all over the carpet soon after breakfast.

But he was creative too. Think of the notorious boat he tried to bomb. Think of the tin bath boat. At least he had had a share in constructing it. Think of Stephen's 'motor-bike'. Think of his rendering of the outside toilet. Not the most engaging of activities, but he pursued it to the very end. He was a devotee of Lego, and made impressively elaborate structures. A tribute to New Mill is that one of his most famous successes was a Lego septic tank. Well, *he* called it a septic tank.

As with Christopher and fishing, Martin discovered wires. I don't think there was any great epiphany; indeed, it is possible to argue that wires and electricity had always been there. New Mill gave him the opportunity to 'do' them.

It is easy to understand how somebody can get aesthetic pleasure out of music or art or Nature or whatever. No doubt a Renaissance architect got a kick out of a cluster of Corinthian columns he had just knocked out. We are told – and we have little choice but to take it on trust, however difficult it may be for us – that a mathematician can get a buzz from a calculus problem, or rather from its solution. Well, Martin could get that sort of pleasure from anything to do with wires. As he grew, and it became clear that he was serious about it, it is only fitting that we now dignify his interests with the name electronics.

The majority of it, in the early days, was self-taught. He just absorbed it as if he were human blotting paper. When he went to secondary school, he used to be approached by members of staff carrying a silent transistor radio with the request that he make it talk again. He usually did.

When he came into possession of a new portable of his own, he carried it round as if it were the Koh-i-noor on a silk cushion, and reverently unwrapped first the cardboard, then the plastic inside, before finally putting it into operation. When he had finished listening, he, equally reverently, reversed the procedure.

The cricket and music critic, Neville Cardus, wrote in his autobiography about a Yorkshire cricketer called Emmott Robinson, who for years was one of the mainstays of his county's bowling attack. So devoted was he to the game and the county that Cardus was constrained to remark, 'I imagine that he was created one day by God scooping up the nearest acre of Yorkshire soil at hand, then breathing on it, and saying, "Now, lad, tha's called Emmott Robinson and tha can go on with new ball at t' pavilion end." ' Well, by the same token, God said to Martin, 'I have put you on this earth to do computers.' And that is what he has done all his life.

He liked doing other things too, but they were mainly of a constructional nature. No art or poetry or cricket or football for Martin. I couldn't help him with electronics because I don't know any, but I thought I might be able to assist in another department.

When he was about nine or ten, I gave him the most creative Christmas present I had ever thought of. It was getting near the day, and I had come up with nothing. I didn't have the resources for colossal kits or vehicles or sets. I knew that, all too often, if I had provided one of these prodigies, it could easily have been taken to bits, and abandoned a few weeks later, or turned into a home-made space-ship.

I was in a Barnstaple builder's yard one day, snuffing the scent of timber, tar, and sawdust, and it hit me. I went to the foreman. Did he by chance have any off-cuts of battening or planking or tongued-and-grooved that were no further use to him? Yes, he did. I came away with an armful, which he refused to take payment for.

That triggered another idea. I repaired to the retail shop and stated my errand. I was buying something for a boy who liked making things. I already had the wood. Would the man be kind enough to show me a selection of nails and screws. (I was perfectly willing to pay.) He picked up a small empty carton, went right along the display of nails and screws, scooping a small handful from every box on show.

'How much?' I said.

He waved it away.

I had anticipated what Martin might do. I didn't wait for him to take something to bits; I simply gave him the bits ready made. I had just bought him the best Christmas present he had ever had from me, and it didn't cost a penny.

Not all the memories were charming ones. One chore the boys didn't like, and I can't say I blame them, was scooping the grass out from between the cobbles in front of the house every summer holidays. I don't think it dragged on all that long, and the job was never completely finished (nothing at New Mill ever was), but it showed that we were prepared to make some effort to keep the wilderness at bay. It was pretty soul-destroying work, but it did give me more time to tackle the endless bramble-bashing, mowing, New Mill Lane hedge-trimming, and general maintenance, which of course became more of a burden in high summer.

We were never flooded, but the stream did rise once or twice. When it did that, it took on a completely aspect – brown, flat, and silent, and sinister. We had no flood defences; all we could do was stand just inside the front door and watch and hope. When it sloshed within a couple of inches of the top of the doorstep, it tended to concentrate the mind somewhat. Worse, you stepped from the doorstep *down* into the lounge, so, if the water had seeped in, there would have been no way we could have simply swept it out.

We were lucky. We were lucky too with the snow; we hardly

had any. Places like New Mill are just the sort of houses that you read about in the papers or see on the local news – five-foot drifts, evocative shots of immobile Land Rovers, miles of snow-drenched landscape, and smoke-breathing TV reporters in enormous scarves and pompoms eagerly puffing information into hand-held microphones – which we could see perfectly well for ourselves.

Well, we escaped that too. I could do nothing about flood preparations, but I could lay in a winter supply of food, and I did. Luckily again, we never had need of it.

It got cold, mind you, and there were some Dickensian frosty scenes like those shown to Scrooge by the Ghost of Christmas Past. When we first had the old Land Rover, I was concerned to make sure that it would start reliably. I knew that my mechanical knowledge would not be equal to the task of persuading it if it played up. It was old, remember, and fragile. Cussed too. So I spoilt it with a hot water bottle, just to put it in a good mood. I used to park it up outside Miss Blackmore's house every night, with a small hurricane lamp suspended under the bonnet. . . Yes, maybe, but it worked. Started every time. Never blew up once.

The frost – and Christmas – produced another challenge, but only for me. I had developed the habit of taking a shower under the waterfall on occasional mornings. Quite natural in the summer, but it could get teeth-grinding in other seasons. However, the feelings of well-being and, above all, of smug superiority it generated made it worthwhile. Not content with that, I resolved to try doing it on Christmas morning. Successfully, I am pleased to add. Flushed with success (if that's the right word), I determined to make it a New Mill tradition. Every Christmas we were there, I took a shower under the waterfall on Christmas morning. The sense of virtue thus engendered would have made anybody a Pharisee.

And so the reminiscences kept coming – the same ones, every time we talked about New Mill. They still do. Like family snaps passed round for the hundredth time.

Tiny ones too: the old Lynton coach road, which was so steep, we were told, that passengers had to get out and walk – even push

219

when necessary. (Yes, I have mentioned it already.) The remains of the narrow-gauge railway which ran from Lynton to Barnstaple. There was a derelict bridge from that railway up at Caffyn's by the top of New Mill Lane, remember? You came across evidence of it all along the line. Outside Lynton is the old railway station, which became a private residence. The owners bought part of the line too, and so can now boast that they own the longest, narrowest garden in England. (I've mentioned that before too.)

The line performed a useful service during most of its life, from 1898 to 1935. Mrs. Hildick used to tell us that she caught the train regularly when she attended school in Barnstaple, and the guard would hold the train for them if he saw them hurrying up the hill. Alas, it fell victim to progress, in the shape of the motor car, and it could not compete. Inevitably there was a well-meaning society of conservationists who tried to save it, but the tide was against them. There was a large protest meeting scheduled in Barnstaple to make an eloquent plea against the closure. A lot of people came. They didn't come from Lynton by train; they all turned up in motor cars. (Did you miss it the first time I told you?)

Incidentally, there is now a company which has re-opened part of the line (steam train and all) round Woody Bay, and has plans to re-open all of it.

Underneath the wooden window-sill in the lounge we found a copper coin – a token, to be precise. Successful entrepreneurs in the Industrial Revolution used to make even more money by paying their employees not in coin of the realm but in tokens, which could be exchanged for goods, but only in the employer's shop. It was a nice littler earner.

This one was minted by John Wilkinson, Iron-Mad Wilkinson they called him. So you can guess what his line of business was. It was a substantial piece of currency – heavier than any coin we have today, heavier than a half-crown (for those with pensioner's memories). Wilkinson was indeed iron-mad. He promoted the first iron bridge, at Coalbrookdale in Shropshire (and it's still there), worked with James Watt on the cylinders of his steam engines, constructed the first iron barge, and had himself buried, so they say, in an iron coffin.

Even tinier snaps remain, flattened like faded flowers in the album of the memory. Whenever I wanted to clean brushes of emulsion paint, all I had to do was leave them in the mill leet. The water was of a shallowness and strength that produced a perfect combination. I could forget about them for a couple of days. It gave me the cleanest paint brushes I have ever had.

The birds – gulls from the coast, magpies, jays, buzzards, robins, crows. The heron I have already mentioned. They were the easy ones. There were plenty of others, but I don't know their names. We have a large garden still, but we don't see the birds we used to.

I improved my repertoire of flower recognition. Primroses of course by the million. Not as big as Cornish primroses, I have to admit. But for sheer profusion unmatchable. On banks and road-sides great clumps of them as big as gangsters' funeral wreaths for their victims. Snowdrops, violets, wild garlic, foxgloves, campion, rose-bay willow herb, speedwell, bindweed, dog-rose, forget-me-not, furze, wild honeysuckle, and so on. Not forgetting the fuchsials and the japonical.

Did we miss it? Do we miss it?

Ah. . . As the visiting expert up on the stage would have said, 'That's a very good question.'

Did we lie awake at nights in School House thinking about it? I doubt it. Wishing we were still there? Good heavens no. Would we, given the choice, do it again? I doubt that too.

However, we all took something away from New Mill. Ask any of us, and we could talk about it very easily – and, if not switched off, at greater length than the questioner would have imagined, or wanted.

For me it has that much in common with two other passages of life that I have been through – National Service, and the War. I can always talk about all three. I am marked by all three. I could never claim that they were enjoyable all the time (anything but sometimes). I wouldn't have missed any of them. I would not like to repeat any of them. But I am glad I have all of them in my bank account of experience. They all did things for me. I can only hope that New Mill did things for Mrs. Coates and all three boys.

I like to think so. It is interesting that, in later years, all three of them have taken their girl friends – later their respective wives – down to see it. Christopher still has my painting of New Mill on the wall of his lounge. Martin says that the experience of it helped to get him through difficult days in the RAF. If Stephen visits, he contrives when possible to spend just an hour or two up on the Moor. He now takes his son James "up auver". So the imprint is there.

If, like the castaway on the famous desert island, I had to choose just one memory to keep me company, I think it would be not a sight or a smell or a feeling, but a sound. It would be the water.

THE END

ACKNOWLEDGEMENTS

I met a lot of people during the time I spent in this cottage, and my experiences of them, obviously, go a long way towards providing the meat for this book. They did not know at the time what they were providing, and neither did I. But it is equally obvious that I could not have written the book without them. Their testimony is going to be that much more genuine and honest because it was involuntary and unconscious. Therefore that much more valuable too.

So, to everybody who spoke to me, did me favours, or came to my rescue, or in any way made my years in New Mill more worthwhile, my thanks.

And of course my thanks too to the editorial triumvirate who take over once I have finished writing the thing: Mark Webb at Paragon Publishing, Yvonne Reed behind her X-ray spectacles at her slip-up-spotting screen, and my son Stephen.

Exmoor stream